Dangerous Decade:
Taiwan's Security and Crisis Management

Brendan Taylor

'In this astute and sophisticated assessment, Brendan Taylor reveals how Taiwan has again become a tinderbox that could easily ignite – through aggressive probing by China, false complacency in Taipei, and periodic provocations by Washington. A sobering study that should be carefully read by all national security cognoscenti.'
David Shambaugh, George Washington University

Dangerous Decade:
Taiwan's Security and Crisis Management

Brendan Taylor

IISS The International Institute for Strategic Studies

The International Institute for Strategic Studies

Arundel House | 6 Temple Place | London | WC2R 2PG | UK

First published September 2019 by **Routledge**
4 Park Square, Milton Park, Abingdon, Oxon, OX14 4RN

for **The International Institute for Strategic Studies**
Arundel House, 6 Temple Place, London, WC2R 2PG, UK
www.iiss.org

Simultaneously published in the USA and Canada by **Routledge**
52 Vanderbilt Avenue, New York, NY 10017

Routledge is an imprint of Taylor & Francis, an Informa Business

© 2019 The International Institute for Strategic Studies

DIRECTOR-GENERAL AND CHIEF EXECUTIVE Dr John Chipman
EDITOR Dr Nicholas Redman
ASSISTANT EDITOR Sam Stocker
EDITORIAL Vivien Antwi, Sara Hussain, Jack May
COVER/PRODUCTION John Buck, Carolina Vargas
COVER IMAGES: Getty

The International Institute for Strategic Studies is an independent centre for research, information and debate on the problems of conflict, however caused, that have, or potentially have, an important military content. The Council and Staff of the Institute are international and its membership is drawn from almost 100 countries. The Institute is independent and it alone decides what activities to conduct. It owes no allegiance to any government, any group of governments or any political or other organisation. The IISS stresses rigorous research with a forward-looking policy orientation and places particular emphasis on bringing new perspectives to the strategic debate.

The Institute's publications are designed to meet the needs of a wider audience than its own membership and are available on subscription, by mail order and in good bookshops. Further details at www.iiss.org.

British Library Cataloguing in Publication Data
A catalogue record for this book is available from the British Library

Library of Congress Cataloging in Publication Data

ADELPHI series
ISSN 1944-5571

ADELPHI 470–471
ISBN 978-0-367-43748-0

Contents

ACKNOWLEDGEMENTS

This book began during a lunchtime conversation in Canberra with Tim Huxley, Executive Director of the IISS–Asia office. I am indebted to Tim for his friendship and mentorship over many years, for his encouragement to write this book, for the countless conversations he endured during its early stages, and for the time and attention he gave to carefully reviewing the final manuscript. Several long conversations with William Choong, also from the IISS–Asia office, were extremely helpful too. Nick Redman, editor of the *Adelphi* series was, as always, a joy to work with. I am also grateful to Sam Stocker for copy-editing the manuscript with care, enthusiasm and evident subject-matter expertise.

Special thanks are due to Richard Rigby, who has taught me more than anyone about China – particularly during the many memorable trips we have shared both there and beyond. His advice and support for this project were indispensable. Many others assisted and inspired along the way, including Michael Wesley, Paul Dibb, Hugh White, Linda Jakobson, Iain Henry, Bill Tow, David Envall, Bates Gill, Michael Cole, Nick Bisley, Sam Roggeveen, Minxin Pei, Rowan Callick, Alexander Neill, Andrew Yang, I-Chung Lai, David Capie, Norah Huang and Feng Zhang.

I would also like to thank the officials from the governments of Australia, Japan, Singapore, Taiwan and the United States, as well as those from the Chinese People's Liberation Army, who shared their perspectives on an anonymous basis.

As ever, this book would not have come to fruition without the unconditional support of my wife Jenny and my mother Marie. I thank them for their love, encouragement and patience. This book is dedicated to my daughters, Sinead and Siobhan. It is the hope that they will never have to endure the horrors of major-power conflict which continues to provide the primary motivation for my work in this field.

ABBREVIATIONS

A2/AD	anti-access and area denial
AIT	American Institute in Taiwan
ARATS	Association for Relations Across the Taiwan Straits
ASW	anti-submarine warfare
BRI	Belt and Road Initiative
C4ISR	command, control, communications, computer, intelligence, surveillance and reconnaissance
CBMs	confidence-building measures
CCP	Chinese Communist Party
CIA	Central Intelligence Agency
CPTPP	Comprehensive and Progressive Agreement for Trans-Pacific Partnership
CUES	Code for Unplanned Encounters at Sea
DMZ	demilitarised zone
DPP	Democratic Progressive Party
IAEA	International Atomic Energy Agency
IDS	Indigenous Defense Submarine
INER	Institute for Nuclear Energy Research
KMT	Kuomintang
NDAA	National Defense Authorization Act
OSCE	Organization for Security and Cooperation in Europe
PLA	People's Liberation Army
PLAAF	People's Liberation Army Air Force
PLAN	People's Liberation Army Navy
PLARF	People's Liberation Army Rocket Force
PRC	People's Republic of China
RIMPAC	*Rim of the Pacific* exercise
ROC	Republic of China
SEF	Straits Exchange Foundation
TRA	Taiwan Relations Act
WHA	World Health Assembly
WHO	World Health Organization

INTRODUCTION

After decades of relative stability, tensions are again building over Taiwan. This book argues that these mark the beginnings of a major strategic crisis. A crisis could erupt suddenly, sparked by an episode of inadvertent escalation – such as the collision of military ships or aircraft operating in the Taiwan Strait. Or pressure could build gradually in the coming months and years, as Beijing and Washington descend deeper into what some strategic commentators are branding a new cold war.[1] Either way, a new crisis over Taiwan would likely be a significantly more serious affair than earlier such episodes in the mid-1950s and mid-1990s. The fate of Taiwan's 23.5 million inhabitants could hang in the balance. Indeed, life as we know it could change dramatically if the coming Taiwan crisis is not prudently managed.

It has become commonplace to lay the blame for growing tensions over Taiwan squarely with Beijing. China's strongman leader, Xi Jinping, has put the island front and centre in his signature 'China Dream' – a vision for making the Middle Kingdom wealthy and powerful again. In a January 2019 address commemorating the 40th anniversary of China's

'Message to Compatriots in Taiwan', Xi delivered a stark message: Taiwan must accept Beijing's preferred 'one country, two systems' model for reunification, or face the military consequences.[2] But China's coercive tactics are part of a larger, more complex picture. Beijing is also reacting to changes on Taiwan, where the passage of seven decades since the Chinese Civil War of 1945–49 has left the island's inhabitants feeling increasingly estranged from the mainland. Taiwan's leader, Tsai Ing-wen, asserts that Xi must 'face the reality' of Taiwan's existence as a free and democratic society.[3] Meanwhile, the Trump administration's erratic policies toward both China and Taiwan contribute an additional layer of unpredictability.

In fact, Beijing, Taipei and Washington are each challenging the cross-strait 'status quo' which until now has, for the most part, kept the peace. That this status quo is unravelling is due to shifts in the underlying balance of military power among them. As the strongest side of this triangle, Washington has traditionally been able to deter Beijing from using force against the island while simultaneously dissuading Taiwan from issuing a formal declaration of independence. But the significant leaps forward that China's military has taken since the mid-1990s have altered that equation. Taiwan could once arguably have held its own in a fight with its much larger neighbour, but the cross-strait military balance is now decisively in China's favour. Meanwhile, although the US would still almost certainly prevail in a conflict with China over Taiwan today – albeit with significantly greater cost and risk than was previously the case – this book argues that its ability to do so is rapidly eroding and will probably be gone within a decade.

As the window on Washington's ability to come to Taiwan's defence closes, the chances of major crisis will intensify. This book identifies several scenarios where Beijing, Taipei and Washington could find themselves climbing the ladder of military escalation. As pragmatic as the Taiwanese have tradi-tionally been, Taipei could inadvertently cross Beijing's often ambiguous 'red lines' and provoke a military response. Military ships and aircraft operating in the increasingly crowded skies and waters around the island could collide or engage in combat. The island could gain renewed strategic significance against the backdrop of deepening Sino-American rivalry, placing Taiwan at the centre of a superpower crisis, just as it was during the 1950s. A crisis over Taiwan could also rapidly escalate, as parties succumb to powerful military-technical incentives to move early.

The policy options for addressing growing tensions over Taiwan are not promising. Wu Den-yih, chairman of Taiwan's opposition Kuomintang (KMT), created contro-versy in February 2019 by suggesting that his party would pursue a peace treaty with the mainland if returned to power in the island's January 2020 elections. But given the widen-ing gulf between Beijing and Taipei, the diplomatic resolution of Taiwan's disputed status remains a long way off. China's preferred 'one country, two systems' formula, for instance, has been resoundingly rejected by both sides of Taiwanese politics, who have witnessed with trepidation Beijing's heavy-handed application of this approach in Hong Kong. A larger US–China deal, where Taiwan ends up as a bargaining chip, remains a possibility. But this too is an unlikely prospect given the increasing strains between Beijing and Washington.

With the growing possibility that these strains might develop into a cold war, calls for the US to deepen ties and to enhance its commitment to Taiwan have grown louder. Options ranging from a more visible US military presence in the waters around Taiwan, through to the sale of more advanced weaponry and the forging of a formal alliance of the kind in place at the height of the Cold War, have all been mooted by commentators and analysts. Tying these options together is the well-intentioned belief that they will enhance deterrence against Chinese coercion or a military attack targeting Taiwan. Yet effective deterrence ultimately rests upon whether Washington can convince Beijing that it is both *willing* and *able* to defend the island. With a president who espouses an 'America First' policy in the White House, one could forgive China's leaders for doubting that Washington would really be willing to accept the costs and risks of coming to Taiwan's aid. Even if it were, the ability of the US to do so is diminishing, as argued in Chapter Two.

Given the stakes and sensitivities involved, Beijing is unlikely to back down, even in the face of enhanced US deterrence. Indeed, this book argues that China's leaders are most likely to respond in kind, thus exacerbating an already worsening Sino-American security dilemma. History tells us that such dynamics often escalate into full-blown conflict. The costs of such a conflict over Taiwan should not be underestimated. As the final chapter of this book details, China's economy would go into freefall – with significant spillover effects for its major trading partners. Chinese cyber attacks alone could cost the US between US$70 billion and US$900bn. This is not to mention the massive loss of human life, especially were conflict to escalate to the nuclear level.

Neither Beijing, Taipei nor Washington want conflict, not least because of the prohibitive costs involved. But rationality does not always prevail in decisions for war. Indeed, as Chapter Three of the book discusses, inadvertent escalation over Taiwan poses the greatest risk to peace during the coming 'dangerous decade'. Unfortunately, continuing political stalemate across the strait inhibits the kinds of crisis-avoidance measures that were discussed so optimistically by scholars and policymakers alike in relation to Taiwan more than a decade ago. Acknowledging this constraint, the book suggests instead the introduction of a narrower set of formal crisis-management mechanisms designed to navigate a major Taiwan crisis.

Writing almost half a century ago, the Australian scholar Coral Bell sagely observed that 'to concede the existence of a conflict is the essential first step to managing the crises to which it gives rise'.[4] This book's primary contention is that the prospects for a Taiwan conflict are real and intensifying. However, they are not yet being treated with the seriousness nor the urgency that they deserve. Unless and until they are, the robust management mechanisms needed to ensure that the next Taiwan crisis does not escalate into catastrophic conflict will not be put in place. While the primary responsibility for doing so rests with Beijing, Taipei and Washington, this is and should be a matter of international concern – for a full-blown Taiwan conflict would have far-reaching ramifications.

CHAPTER ONE

A shifting status quo

Since Chiang Kai-shek's retreat to the island in 1949, Taiwan has been the focus of three international crises – in 1954–55, 1958 and 1995–96. But major conflict has thus far been avoided. Peace has been preserved through a deceptively simple arrangement known as the cross-strait 'status quo'. This term encompasses a series of tacit commitments made by Beijing, Taipei and Washington to maintain stability across the strait, until such time as a peaceful and more permanent solution to the so-called 'Taiwan problem' could be found. Provided Taiwan did not issue a formal declaration of independence, Beijing for decades was largely resigned to its inability to reincorporate the island militarily. Taipei, in turn, committed to living with a political status short of formal statehood so as not to provoke a Chinese military attack. The US sought to preserve this uneasy equilibrium, both through deterring Chinese military action and by dissuading Taiwan from a declaration of independence that would trigger it.

The cross-strait status quo is vague. A leading authority on cross-strait relations, June Teufel Dreyer, characterised it as a 'largely meaningless phrase and a dangerous ambiguity'.[1] Yet it is the very flexibility of this construct that has traditionally appealed most to policymakers. As this chapter shows, Taipei, Beijing and Washington have advanced differing interpretations of the cross-strait status quo. Moreover, these definitions have evolved over time, often directly in response to definitional shifts from at least one of the other parties. However, this approach is no longer sustainable. All three capitals are currently challenging the status quo, pushing it in increasingly divergent and, indeed, incompatible directions. Writing a decade ago, Teufel Dryer asserted that 'there is no status quo on the issue of China and Taiwan, nor has one ever existed'.[2] Should present trends continue, this once controversial claim could well become conventional wisdom.

The view from Taipei

Taiwan has been subject to numerous claims over the course of its turbulent history. The Dutch East India Company administered the island for a short period during the seventeenth century (1624–62), for instance, at China's suggestion. The Chinese warlord Zheng Chenggong subsequently seized the island and used it as a base for waging a campaign against China's ruling Qing dynasty. The Qing prevailed over Zheng in 1683, however, and for the next two centuries ruled the island. As other foreign powers, namely France and Japan, began occupying parts of Taiwan in the late 1800s, the Qing formally recognised the island as a province of China. As part of the price for their humiliating defeat in the Sino-Japanese War of 1894–95, however, the Qing were forced to cede the island to Imperial Japan under the terms of the Treaty of Shimonoseki. This ushered in four decades of Japanese colonisation, during which time the island also underwent important economic, social, infrastructural and technological reforms.[3]

When the Second World War ended, China – then known as the Republic of China (ROC) – was ruled by the Nationalist Party (Kuomintang or KMT). China had fought on the side of the victors and its leader, General Chiang Kai-shek, successfully made the case that Taiwan should be returned to the control of the mainland. China was soon embroiled in civil war, however, in which Chiang's forces – severely weakened by the conflict against the Japanese from 1937 to 1945 – were defeated. Chiang and his remaining troops retreated to Taiwan, where they re-established the ROC. The KMT pledged to reclaim the mainland from the Chinese Communist Party (CCP), which in 1949 established the People's Republic of China (PRC) under the leadership of Mao Tse-tung.

The KMT imposed martial law on Taiwan in May 1949, a situation that would remain in effect for 38 years. This was justified on two grounds. Firstly, the island faced the threat of imminent attack from the mainland and was thus, in effect, in a state of emergency. Secondly, because the KMT claimed to be the legitimate ruler of all of China, government had to be suspended until elections could be held on the mainland.[4] Chiang's rule started out as repressively as the half-century of Japanese colonisation that had preceded it. Already in February 1947, prior to his retreat, Chiang had famously ordered the suppression of an uprising that resulted in the indiscriminate slaughter of thousands of the island's residents. The anti-KMT embitterment generated by this episode lingered among Taiwan's locals for decades to come. So too did Chiang's fears of sedition. He put his son, Chiang Ching-kuo, in charge of internal security. In this capacity, Chiang the younger carried out a ruthless purge that came to be known as the 'White Terror'.[5]

The legitimacy of KMT rule was increasingly called into question, however, as Taiwan's international position weakened. In October 1971, the ROC lost its seat at the United

Nations to the PRC. By decade's end, most countries had responded to this development by switching diplomatic recognition from Taipei to Beijing. Most importantly, as a product of the historic normalisation in Sino-US relations – which unfolded throughout the 1970s and officially came into effect on 1 January 1980 – Washington de-recognised Taiwan. Although the KMT continued to maintain its right to govern all of China, the credibility of this claim sharply diminished in light of these developments.

Chiang died in 1975 and was succeeded by his son. Significantly, Chiang Ching-kuo recognised that continued KMT rule hinged upon the party's ability to reflect the will of the Taiwanese people. By this time, the island had developed into a relatively prosperous and increasingly well-educated society. While Chiang was certainly not as committed to democracy as the founding father of the KMT, Sun Yat-sen – who was a key figure in the overthrow of the Qing dynasty and served as the ROC's first provisional president (1911–12), and who envisaged China's eventual democratisation following an initial period of Party rule – he did recognise that greater political liberalisation was necessary to stave off a major political crisis. Although he did not completely relinquish the use of repressive techniques, Chiang Ching-kuo relied gradually less upon these than his father. In October 1986, less than two years before his death, Chiang even allowed the formation of an opposition party – the Democratic Progressive Party (DPP) – with the aim of maintaining stability within a Taiwanese society that was growing wealthier, better educated, more cosmopolitan and hungrier for political liberalisation. He also announced his intention to lift martial law.[6]

Chiang's deputy, a Taiwan-born academic named Lee Teng-hui, assumed the leadership of the KMT and continued this program of liberalisation. On 23 March 1996, Lee became the island's first democratically elected president, securing 54% of the popular vote. This democratisation of Taiwan had important internal and external ramifications for the cross-strait status quo. Externally, it significantly enhanced Taiwan's international image. This was particularly so given that it was occurring against the backdrop of the June 1989 Tiananmen Square massacre, which placed Beijing's repressive policies and practices in the international spotlight.[7]

On the island, Chiang the younger's reforms significantly broadened the political spectrum. Views previously regarded as taboo were expressed more openly. In the early 1990s, for instance, the DPP stated that its fundamental goals included the establishment of Taiwan as an independent country and the drafting of a new constitution. By the end of the decade, the DPP's position was that Taiwan was already an independent state and that this reality could only be changed via a national plebiscite. The KMT, on the other hand, maintained its stance that there was only one China: the ROC. Hence, two competing conceptions of the cross-strait status quo had developed on the island.

From the mid-1990s, a more distinct sense of 'Taiwanese' identity also gradually started to emerge. The Election Study Center at Taiwan's National Chengchi University started polling on this issue in 1992. In the first of these polls, 46.4% of respondents indicated that they regarded themselves as 'both Taiwanese and Chinese', 25.5% said they were 'Chinese' and 17.6% identified as 'Taiwanese'. By contrast, in their June 2019 poll, 56.9% of respondents identified as 'Taiwanese', 36.5% as 'both Taiwanese and Chinese' and a mere 3.6% as 'Chinese'.[8] Consistent with these trends, a July 2019 Taiwan Foundation for Democracy poll found that 68.2% of respondents were willing to defend the island if Beijing sought to annex Taiwan by force.[9]

Such views are most pronounced among Taiwan's younger generation. According to recent polling, 100% of those under the age of 29 see themselves as 'exclusively Taiwanese'.[10] This result is unsurprising given that many in this age bracket were born on the island. Unlike their grandparents, they have little or no affinity with the mainland having never lived there. This generation is also ostensibly more willing to defend Taiwan from Chinese aggression. According to another recent Taiwan Foundation for Democracy poll, for instance, 70.3% of those under 40 years of age would be willing to fight for Taiwan should Beijing attempt forceful reunification. Consistent with this, an even higher 73.3% of Taiwanese in this demographic category indicated their opposition to unification with the mainland, even if China were to become a democratic country.[11]

Taiwan's leaders have had to acknowledge these shifting sentiments. Lee Teng-hui, his KMT credentials notwithstanding, provoked Beijing's ire during an interview in July 1999 in which he described cross-strait ties as 'a special state-to-state relationship'.[12] Lee's successor, Chen Shui-bian, went further still. The first DPP president, Chen sought to send a message of reassurance across the strait in his inaugural address. Provided Beijing ruled out the use of force against the island, Chen pledged that he would not declare independence, change Taiwan's name, include Lee's 'state-to-state theory' in the constitution, nor endorse a referendum on altering the cross-strait status quo. However, in August 2002 – two years into his first term – Chen publicly stated his belief that China and Taiwan were separate countries and called for a referendum to decide Taiwan's future.[13] Chen subsequently initiated referendums to coincide with Taiwan's 2004 and 2008 presidential elections. The first dealt with cross-strait issues and the second asked whether the government should seek to re-join the United Nations under the name of Taiwan. These referendums were ultimately declared invalid due to a low voter-response rate. In January 2006, however, Chen did succeed in terminating Taiwan's National Unification Council – a government agency established in 1990 to promote reintegration of the mainland into the ROC.[14]

The election of the KMT's Ma Ying-jeou as president in March 2008 considerably eased cross-strait tensions. Relations between Taiwan and the mainland deepened considerably during his two terms in office. A total of 23 cross-strait agreements were forged in this period, including the high-profile preferential trade agreement known as the 'Economic Cooperation Framework Agreement', signed in June 2010. Direct flights linking Taiwan with the mainland were implemented and Chinese tourism to the island boomed.[15] In September 2015, Ma became the first Taiwanese leader to meet his Chinese counterpart, Xi Jinping, in Singapore. Reflecting the uneasy status quo between Taiwan and China, however, they greeted one another simply as *'xiansheng'* (meaning 'mister') to avoid diplomatic complexities.[16]

A range of domestic factors – including Taiwan's stagnating economy, rising labour prices and a growing gap between rich and poor – contributed to the defeat of KMT candidate Eric Chu in Taiwan's January 2016 presidential elections. Yet Ma's perceived closeness to the mainland also played a part. The so-called 'Sunflower Movement' – a term used to describe large-scale demonstrations by Taiwanese students and civic groups, which occupied Taiwan's parliament from 18 March– 10 April 2014 to protest the island's growing dependence upon the mainland – was a harbinger, while also highlighting the dangers of not being sufficiently attentive to shifting sentiments on the island.[17]

In January 2016, Tsai Ing-wen was elected president of Taiwan in a landslide victory that also saw the DPP take control of the island's legislature for the first time. In her inauguration address, Tsai sought to reassure the mainland – just as her DPP predecessor Chen had done. She observed, for instance, that 'the stable and peaceful development of the cross-strait relationship must be continuously promoted', based upon 'existing realities and political foundations' – including 'the existing Republic of China constitutional order'.[18] Yet Beijing had made clear in the months leading to Tsai's inauguration that it expected her to more clearly commit to the terms of the so-called '1992 Consensus', just as Ma had done. This was an agreement allegedly reached in Hong Kong between two semi-official organisations negotiating on behalf of their governments – the Straits Exchange Foundation (SEF) of Taiwan and the Association for Relations Across the Taiwan Straits (ARATS) of China. It purportedly holds that there is only 'one China', even if both sides have differing interpretations of it.[19] As leader of the independence-leaning DPP, however, it would be politically untenable for Tsai to unambiguously support this consensus.[20] Indeed, unlike the KMT, Tsai and her party maintain that the '1992 Consensus' never existed.[21]

Taiwan nonetheless has a reputation for pragmatism when it comes to the issue of independence. In a public-opinion poll conducted by Taiwan's Mainland Affairs Council in August 2018, for instance, 85.8% of respondents indicated that they were in favour of maintaining the cross-strait status quo.[22] Yet in a November 2016 poll conducted by the Election Study Center, 72% of respondents agreed with the statement that 'Taiwan is an independent country under the name Republic of China'.[23] In other words, an overwhelming majority of the island's population of 23.5 million are of the view that Taiwan is already independent and that this constitutes the current cross-strait status quo.

The DPP received an unexpected drubbing in local elections held in November 2018. Tsai's cross-strait policies arguably played little role in this outcome, which can be better understood as the product of domestic factors – such as ongoing voter dissatisfaction with the state of Taiwan's economy.[24] Nonetheless, Tsai has come under considerable pressure due to this electoral defeat. She resigned as chair of the DPP, and speculation grew that she would not be nominated as her party's candidate for Taiwan's 2020 presidential election.

While Tsai has earned a reputation for measured pragmatism as far as cross-strait relations are concerned, she responded to these pressures by pushing the traditional status quo even harder. In January 2019, for instance, Tsai publicly rejected the 1992 Consensus and asserted that Beijing 'must recognise the island's existence' – including its 'freedom and democracy'.[25] In March 2019, Tsai's National Security Council unveiled measures explicitly designed to counter Xi's preferred 'one country, two systems' formula, while during the same month Tsai also pledged to assist Taiwanese firms currently based on the mainland to return home and to expand their 'global reach'.[26] This latter step was particularly significant, as those firms have traditionally been seen to add economic ballast to the often politically difficult cross-strait relationship. In May 2019, Tsai's foreign minister Joseph Wu – an advocate of Taiwanese independence – also tweeted that 'Democratic #Taiwan is a country in itself & has nothing to do with authoritarian #China'.[27]

Further fuelling China's view that the Tsai administration is incrementally shifting the status quo, she has been accused by Beijing of taking too flexible an approach toward the island's so-called 'de-Sinicization' – including, for instance, the downgrading of elements of Chinese history in school textbooks[28] – and of being too lenient toward pro-independence elements within her government, such as premier William Lai, who repeatedly described himself from April 2018 as a 'Taiwan independence worker' before finally leaving the post in January 2019.[29] Reflecting the internal pressures that Tsai is under, however, Lai subsequently challenged her for the DPP's nomination in the 2020 presidential election, but was defeated by 8.19% (35.67% to 27.48%) in the party's June 2019 primary.[30]

The view from Beijing

China's position on Taiwan's status is clear cut. Beijing sees today's 'Taiwan problem' as a remnant of the Chinese Civil War. When the PRC was established at the culmination of that conflict, Beijing maintained that the government established by the victorious Communists became – in the words of a February 2000 official White Paper – 'the only legal government of the whole of China and its sole legal representative in the international arena, thereby bringing the historical status of the Republic of China to an end'.[31] According to this perspective, the newly established PRC exercised sovereignty over all of the territory previously governed by the ROC, including Taiwan – which was described as being 'an inalienable part of China' and a mere 'local authority in Chinese territory'.[32] This version of the status quo is commonly referred to as the 'one China' principle.

While pledging unswerving adherence to this principle, Beijing over the decades has displayed some flexibility towards its interpretation and implementation. During the 1950s, Mao, for instance, wanted to 'liberate' Taiwan by military means. He tasked the People's Liberation Army (PLA) with drawing up detailed plans to achieve this aim. Yet Mao was equally aware of China's inability to take the island by force, particularly given the likelihood of US involvement in a cross-strait conflict. He thus spent much of the 1950s attempting to exploit tensions in the US–Taiwan relationship, initiating two cross-strait crises designed to test US resolve.[33] Unable to prise open fissures between Taipei and Washington sufficiently, however, and increasingly resigned to the fact that the PLA's limitations precluded China from taking the island by force, Mao turned increasingly to the notion of Taiwan's 'peaceful liberation'. He recognised that this would be a longer-term proposition for the mainland; so much so that in the early 1970s Mao even suggested that China could wait a hundred years for this issue to be resolved.[34]

This emphasis upon patience and 'peaceful unification' became a hallmark of China's Taiwan policy under Mao's successor, Deng Xiaoping. Deng believed that time was on China's side, famously suggesting that reunification could wait up to a thousand years. He maintained that Beijing's ability to achieve this outcome would improve as China's own power increased. In his terms, 'whether we can bring Taiwan to the embrace of the motherland and achieve national reunification depends on how well we handle our own business … If we fare well with respect to modernization and economic development, we will have a greater power for achieving reunification.'[35] Deng was not suggesting here that a wealthier China would be able to develop the armed forces needed to conquer Taiwan (although he and his successors refused to rule out this possibility). Rather, he believed that the island would eventually be drawn into the orbit of a more economically powerful China. Towards this end, Deng advocated the development of deeper economic interdependencies between China and Taiwan that would serve both to dampen political animosities between the two sides while simultaneously binding the island into Beijing's preferred one China framework.

Consistent with this approach, China's leaders have historically demonstrated a willingness to offer their Taiwanese counterparts a variety of concessions and incentives in support of the one China principle. In 1956, for instance, Chinese premier Zhou Enlai conveyed the message, through a secret emissary dispatched by Chiang Kai-shek and his son, that they would be appointed to senior positions in the Chinese government following Taiwan's 'return to the motherland'.[36] Perhaps the most prominent example of this technique, however, was Deng's 'one country, two systems' approach. Deng's proposal – ultimately applied to facilitate the return of Hong Kong to PRC rule in 1997 – was originally advanced with Taiwan in mind. Under this arrangement, Taiwan would be incorporated into China as a 'special administrative region'. It would be allowed to retain a high level of autonomy, including its capitalist economic system, its own administrative and legislative powers, an independent judiciary and even its own armed forces. Taiwan would also be permitted some autonomy over its foreign affairs, such as the conclusion of commercial and cultural agreements with other countries. Under the 'one country, two systems' approach, Taiwan would also need to recognise Beijing as China's central government and to cede overall responsibility for foreign policy to the mainland.[37]

While Beijing has traditionally viewed the US as the central impediment to its realisation of one China, China's leaders have also shown some willingness to co-opt the US into jointly managing the 'Taiwan problem'. The clearest examples of this occurred during the presidency of Chen Shui-bian (2000–08), when Beijing arrived at the view that its best prospects for reining in what it saw as Chen's secessionist agenda lay in getting the US to exert pressure on Taipei. China's leaders recognised that the paramount interest of the US in this dispute was the maintenance of peace and stability across the Taiwan Strait. Beijing therefore claimed that Washington's interests in a peaceful resolution were analogous to its own, and that there existed considerable common ground between them. At the same time, Beijing also publicly called upon the US to take 'concrete actions' to rein in Chen's 'separatist activities'.[38] For instance, during a November 2003 interview with the *Washington Post* – his first in the Western media – Chinese premier Wen Jiabao expressed hope that 'the U.S. government will recognize the gravity and danger of the provocative remarks and actions taken by the leader of the Taiwan authorities [*sic*] that would undermine the prospects for peaceful reunification and that the U.S. side would not send any wrong signals to the Taiwan authorities'. Moreover, Wen added, 'the U.S. side must be crystal clear in opposing … all other tactics used by the leader of Taiwan authorities to pursue his separatist agenda'.[39]

Despite its professed desire for peaceful reunification, Beijing has consistently refused to rule out the use of military force against Taiwan. Indeed, in March 2005 – in direct response to Chen's provocations – China's tenth National People's Congress formally adopted a new 'Anti-Secession Law'. The key clause of this legislation (Article 8) states that:

> In the event that the 'Taiwan independence' secessionist forces should act under any name or by any means to cause the fact of Taiwan's secession from China, or that major incidents entailing Taiwan's secession from China should occur, or that possibilities for a peaceful reunification should be completely exhausted, the state shall employ non-peaceful means and other necessary measures to protect China's sovereignty and territorial integrity.[40]

Where Mao had initially intended to employ military means to 'liberate' Taiwan, here China was threatening the use of force to prevent Taipei achieving *de jure* independence from the mainland. In other words, Beijing was threatening the use of force to preserve what it regarded as an imperfect status quo.

Unlike in Taiwan, where the cross-strait status quo remains hotly contested, in China the range of opinions is considerably narrower. If there are differences, they exist over how quickly Beijing should push for Taiwan's reunification. The US-based China analyst Denny Roy identifies two dominant schools of thinking. A 'patient' school continues to adhere to Deng's approach, maintaining that time is on China's side and that Taiwan's separatist tendencies can best be countered through efforts to deepen cross-strait integration and trust. An opposing 'impatient' school holds that the island's affinity with the PRC is rapidly evaporating, that Taiwan's separation from the mainland is imminent, and that Beijing should thus be pushing harder for Taipei to make political concessions. Roy observes that the advantage in China's internal debate has swung back and forth between these opposing camps and is largely contingent upon the perceived trajectory of pro-independence activities in Taiwan. In his terms,

> if there is no pro-independence momentum and the economic and social connections are increasing, Beijing can be relatively relaxed and patient. If, however, the island seems to be drifting toward independence, the military coercion component of PRC policy comes to the fore. Belligerent statements by Chinese leaders become sharper and more frequent, accompanied by visible PLA activities with obvious application to a cross-strait war scenario.[41]

Under Xi's leadership, the 'impatient' school appears in the ascendency. Unlike his predecessors, who stated that resolution of the 'Taiwan problem' could wait a hundred or even a thousand years, Xi asserted during the first year of his presidency that the two sides must 'reach a final resolution' and that the issue 'cannot be passed on from generation to generation'.[42] Perhaps most importantly, Xi has made Taiwan a centrepiece of his so-called 'China Dream' – a vision for making the Middle Kingdom once again wealthy and powerful, with a view to ensuring that it never again suffers the ignominy experienced during the so-called 'century of humiliation' (1839–1945) when China was carved up by foreign powers.

Some analysts have suggested that Xi will move to reunify Taiwan as early as 2021, to realise the first of the China Dream's two 'centenary goals'. The CCP celebrates its hundredth anniversary that year and Xi has pledged to build China as a 'moderately prosperous society' by this time. Others argue that his implied deadline for reunification is 2049, the year in which the PRC itself turns 100 and when Xi has committed to building China into 'a great modern socialist country that is prosperous, strong, democratic, culturally advanced and harmonious'.[43]

Either way, Xi has been markedly tougher in his rhetoric on Taiwan than any of his predecessors. In a speech to China's October 2017 National Party Congress, for instance, Xi received rapturous applause when he stated that 'we have the resolve, the confidence, and the ability to defeat separatists' attempts for "Taiwan independence" in any form ... We will never allow anyone, any organization, or any political party, at any time or in any form, to separate any part of Chinese territory from China!'[44] Xi took a similarly uncompromising line when addressing the March 2018 National People's Congress, asserting that Taiwanese separatism 'will be condemned by the Chinese people and punished by history'. 'China has the will, confidence and ability to defeat any separatist activity', Xi declared, while 'the Chinese people share a common belief that it is never allowed and it is absolutely impossible to separate any inch of our great country's territory from China'.[45]

Other major Chinese government statements have reinforced these sentiments. In a speech at the IISS Shangri-La Dialogue in Singapore in June 2019, for instance, Chinese State Councillor and Minister of National Defence General Wei Fenghe delivered an ominous message: 'The US is indivisible and so is China. China must be and will be reunified. We find no excuse not to do so. If anyone dares to split Taiwan from China, the Chinese military has no choice but to fight at all costs for national unity.'[46] In a similar vein, China's July 2019 Defence White Paper charges that

> the fight against separatists is becoming more acute. The Taiwan authorities, led by the Democratic Progressive Party (DPP), stubbornly stick to 'Taiwan independence' and refuse to recognize the 1992 Consensus, which embodies the one-China principle. They have gone further down the path of separatism by stepping up efforts to sever the connection with the mainland in favour of gradual independence, pushing for *de jure* independence, intensifying hostility and confrontation, and borrowing the strength of foreign influence. The 'Taiwan independence' separatist forces and their actions remain the gravest immediate threat to peace and stability in the Taiwan Strait.[47]

As the next chapter goes on to document, Xi has backed these words with actions, using an expanding coercive toolbox of economic, diplomatic and military measures against Taiwan. His growing willingness to threaten the use of force presents yet another challenge to the cross-strait status quo. Just as significantly, Beijing's ability to engage in co-management of the Taiwan issue with Washington has also diminished, as the larger US–China relationship enters an era of deeper strategic competition. Any glimmers of such cooperation – a prominent feature of relations between Beijing and Washington during the presidencies of Hu Jintao and George W. Bush – are now faint. In a lengthy February 2017 phone call with his Chinese counterpart, US President Donald Trump did commit 'at Xi's request' to honour the one China policy.[48] But the subsequent actions of Trump's administration appear to be walking back from that commitment.

The view from Washington

Of the three capitals covered in this chapter, Washington's approach to the cross-strait status quo has arguably changed most often. During the Chinese Civil War, the US initially supported the KMT. It opposed the fracturing of China throughout the first half of the twentieth century – fearing that foreign powers were carving up the Middle Kingdom to their own economic advantage and to the detriment of US companies.[49] Chiang Kai-shek's attempts to reunify China thus appealed to Washington. The ROC also fought on the Allied side during the Second World War. Thus, when US president Franklin D. Roosevelt met with Chiang Kai-shek and British prime minister Winston Churchill in Cairo in late 1943, they agreed that Taiwan should be returned to the mainland when the war ended.

US backing for the KMT, however, was not unconditional. Washington in its August 1949 'China White Paper' came to the conclusion that Chiang's regime was too corrupt and too inept to defeat the Communists, leading it to withdraw all financial and military support in January 1950.[50] President Harry Truman was also concerned that US support for the KMT would motivate the newly established PRC and the Soviet Union to align.[51] In January 1950, secretary of state Dean Acheson also famously delivered a speech before the National Press Club outlining a new American 'defensive perimeter' for Asia that ran from the Philippines, through the Ryukyu Islands, to Japan and the Aleutians.[52] This 'Acheson line' line pointedly left out Taiwan and Korea. Some historians suggest that this latter omission was a key factor in Josef Stalin's decision to give North Korean leader Kim Il-sung the 'green light' to invade the South.[53] Fearing that this development was part of a larger communist offensive into Asia, Truman ordered the US Seventh Fleet to 'neutralize' the Taiwan Strait, thus essentially denying Mao the option of taking the island by force.

The US subsequently stood by Chiang in the two Taiwan Strait crises of the 1950s. Indeed, during the first Taiwan Strait crisis of 1954–55, US president Dwight Eisenhower and his secretary of state John Foster Dulles each publicly threatened to use tactical nuclear weapons in Taiwan's defence.[54] The US and Taiwan also signed a 'Mutual Defense Treaty' – much to Beijing's chagrin – during this episode. Inked in December 1954 and ratified the following year, the language of the treaty was similar to that used in other alliances the US forged with Asian countries in the early 1950s – especially its clause that 'each party recognises that an armed attack in the West Pacific Area directed against the territories of either of the parties would be dangerous to its own peace and safety and that it would act to meet the common danger in accordance with its constitutional processes'.[55] For the next two decades, Taiwan became a leading recipient of American economic aid, receiving approximately US$100m in assistance per year from 1951–64.[56] The US armed forces – having formally re-established ties with their Taiwanese counterparts – also established a sizeable presence on the island.[57]

Washington turned away from Taiwan once more during the 1970s, however, as president Richard Nixon and his national security advisor Henry Kissinger saw the potential for Sino-American alignment to tilt the Cold War balance of power decisively in America's favour. Beijing made US de-recognition of Taiwan a requirement of this new Sino-American bargain. In the three communiqués that followed in 1972, 1978 and 1982 – which provided the foundation for normalising US–China relations – Washington equivocated. It adopted a new one China policy, which acknowledged Beijing's one China principle without formally endorsing it. The first of these communiqués – the so-called 'Shanghai Communiqué' – stated that 'The United States acknowledges that all Chinese on either side of the Taiwan Strait maintain there is but one China and that Taiwan is a part of China. The United States Government does not challenge that position.'[58] Likewise, the 1978 Communiqué establishing diplomatic relations between the US and the PRC outlined that 'The United States of America recognizes the Government of the People's Republic of China as the sole legal government of China. Within this context, the people of the United States will maintain cultural, commercial and other unofficial relations with the people of Taiwan … The Government of the United States of America acknowledges the Chinese position that there is but one China and Taiwan is part of China.'[59]

Influential members of the US Congress were disgruntled that the Carter administration did not consult them sufficiently as it completed the formalities of Sino-American normalisation. Although some of these lawmakers were genuinely supportive of Taiwan and sympathetic to its plight, normalisation had also occurred in the immediate aftermath of the Vietnam War – a time when Congress was determined to assert itself more forcefully in the realm of foreign policy.[60] In 1979, Congress thus passed the Taiwan Relations Act (TRA) stipulating how the US would maintain security ties with the island following US–China normalisation. Three requirements stood out: firstly, the TRA noted that 'any effort to determine the future of Taiwan by other than peaceful means, including by boycotts or embargoes, [is] a threat to the peace and security of the Western Pacific area and of grave concern to the United States'. Secondly, it committed the US to 'provid[ing] Taiwan with arms of a defensive character'. And thirdly, it required maintenance of 'the capacity of the United States to resist any resort to force or other forms of coercion that would jeopardize the security, or the social or economic system, of the people on Taiwan'.[61]

The TRA's coexistence with the 1972 and 1978 communiqués introduced a new level of ambiguity into US policy on Taiwan. This deepened further in August 1982, when the Reagan administration signed a third communiqué addressing the thorny issue of US arms sales to Taiwan. This third communiqué stated that the US 'does not seek to carry out a long-term policy of arms sales to Taiwan, that its arms sales to Taiwan will not exceed, either in qualitative or quantitative terms, the level of those supplied in recent years since the establishment of diplomatic relations between the United States and China, and that it intends gradually to reduce its sale of arms to Taiwan'.[62] These commitments seemed to directly contravene the TRA.

Washington, however, opted to utilise this 'strategic ambiguity' to support the cross-strait status quo as part of an approach that came to be known as 'dual deterrence'.[63] On the one hand, the fact that the TRA left open the possibility of the US coming to Taiwan's defence could still deter a Chinese attack against the island. At the same time, the lack of any ironclad commitment that such support would be forthcoming might also serve to rein in reckless Taiwanese behaviour. As James Baker, Reagan's secretary of state, once observed, if we said we would come to the defense of Taiwan under any and all circumstances, she would declare independence and China would move – no doubt about that in my mind. If we said we wouldn't China would move. And so we shouldn't say under what circumstances and to what extent we will aid Taiwan, but we should make it clear that we would view with the gravest concern any resort to the use of force.[64]

In keeping with this approach, the US has subsequently approved the sale of major weapons platforms to Taiwan. The first of these approvals occurred in the lead-up to the 1992 presidential election, when US president George H.W. Bush – partly also for domestic political reasons – agreed to the sale of 150 F-16 fighter aircraft to Taiwan. Bush's son, George W. Bush, also approved a major arms sale to Taiwan early in his presidency, which included four decommissioned *Kidd*-class destroyers, 12 P3-C *Orion* anti-submarine and maritime-patrol aircraft, and eight diesel-electric submarines. Beijing considered the latter 'offensive' rather than 'defensive' weaponry, meaning that their transfer violated the spirit if not the letter of the TRA. Just as significantly, however, George W. Bush also moved away from the two-decades-old practice of discussing Taiwan's weapons requests annually to holding these on an 'as-needed' basis.[65] This created some defence-budgeting and -planning difficulties for the island by making the timing of major arms procurements less predictable.[66] Despite this change in practice, however, the Obama administration approved the sale of approximately US$14 billion-worth of weaponry to Taiwan – more than that approved by all previous American presidents since 1979 combined.[67]

As during the 1950s, the US has also come to Taiwan's defence during moments of crisis. Most notably, in March 1996 the Clinton administration deployed two aircraft-carrier battle groups to the Taiwan Strait after China conducted large-scale military exercises – involving 260 aircraft, 40 ships and 150,000 troops in Fujian province directly opposite Taiwan – and test-fired missiles near the island's two largest commercial ports, Kaohsiung.[68] These military exercises and missile tests took place in the run-up to Taiwan's first direct presidential election, apparently with the aim of intimidating voters. They appear to have had the opposite effect, with analysts estimating that Beijing's coercive tactics gave the ultimate victor, Lee Teng-hui, a 5% boost in the March 1996 poll.[69]

Although the US also began covertly readying weapons, making contingency plans and preparing batteries of *Patriot* missiles for transfer to Taiwan, the prospect of full-blown conflict was reportedly not considered a serious possibility at the time. Nonetheless, the Clinton administration believed that the credibility of the US as the region's security guarantor was being challenged. In response, its dispatching of carriers was at that time the largest US naval deployment to Asia since the end of the Vietnam War.[70]

In April 2001, early during his first term in office, Bush expressed a similar willingness to support Taiwan when he stated during a live television interview that the US would do 'whatever it took to help Taiwan defend theirself' in the event of a Chinese attack.[71] Yet Bush also showed a clear willingness to rein in Taiwanese behaviour which threatened the cross-strait status quo. In early December 2003, for instance, he reportedly sent a secret envoy to meet with Chen, to convey US opposition to his holding of referendums steering the island in the direction of independence.[72] Several days later, Bush hosted Chinese premier Wen Jiabao at the White House and observed publicly that 'the comments and actions made by the leader of Taiwan indicate that he may be willing to make decisions unilaterally to change the status quo, which we oppose'.[73] The following April, Bush's assistant secretary of state for East Asian and Pacific affairs, James Kelly, then delivered perhaps the strongest ever public rebuke from a US government official against Taiwan when he said that

> A unilateral move toward independence will avail Taiwan of nothing it does not already enjoy in terms of democratic freedom, autonomy, prosperity, and security. Realistically, such moves carry the potential for a response from the P.R.C. ... that could destroy much of what Taiwan has built and crush its hopes for the future ... We, in the United States, see these risks clearly and trust they are well understood by President Chen Shui-bian and others in Taiwan.[74]

As in so many areas, Trump has largely torn up this traditional diplomatic playbook on Taiwan. Immediately following his election in November 2016, he became the first US president or president-elect since normalisation to speak directly with Taiwan's leader, when he took a congratulatory phone call from Tsai.[75] After his inauguration in January 2017, Trump publicly asserted that the one China policy was up for negotiation, before confirming the following month that he would honour this policy 'at Xi's request' and not speak with Tsai again by phone without first consulting his Chinese counterpart.[76]

In fairness to Trump, he has had to contend with a Congress where both anti-China and pro-Taiwan sentiment are clearly on the rise. In early 2018, for instance, both the House of Representatives and the Senate passed the Taiwan Travel Act, allowing officials at all levels of the US government to meet with their Taiwanese counterparts. Trump could have simply allowed this non-binding bill to go into effect without his signature, but he angered Beijing when he opted instead to sign it into law in March 2018.[77] In a similar vein, Congress in its 2019 National Defense Authorization Act (NDAA) – the legislation specifying the annual budget and expenditures for the Department of Defense – required the secretary of defense to conduct an assessment of Taiwan's armed forces within 12 months. The NDAA also reaffirmed the TRA, and recommended closer defence and security cooperation with Taiwan, improved predictability of US arms sales to the island, and exchanges of senior defence officials and military officers.[78] In perhaps the boldest pro-Taiwan move to date from congressional quarters, however, five prominent Republican senators wrote to House Speaker Nancy Pelosi in February 2019 requesting that she invite Tsai to address a joint meeting of Congress. The proposal generated considerable debate.[79] When Pelosi and Tsai spoke by phone in April 2019 –Taiwan's president was transiting through Hawaii at the time, en route back from visiting the island's Pacific allies – they reportedly did not discuss the matter.[80]

The Trump administration appears to have needed little encouragement to launch its own series of pro-Taiwan initiatives. Its statements have also been strongly supportive of the island. The December 2017 US National Security Strategy, for example, stated for the first time that 'we will maintain our strong ties with Taiwan in accordance with our "One China" policy, including our commitments under the Taiwan Relations Act to provide for Taiwan's legitimate defense needs and deter coercion'.[81] Then-secretary of defense James Mattis echoed these sentiments, stressing the United States' commitment to Taiwan in both his 2017 and 2018 addresses at the IISS Shangri-La Dialogue in Singapore.[82] So too did National Security Advisor John Bolton – a long-time supporter of Taiwan – when in

April 2019 he tweeted: 'Chinese military provocations won't win any hearts and minds in Taiwan, but they will strengthen the resolve of people everywhere who value democracy. The Taiwan Relations Act (TRA) and our commitment are clear.'[83] In June 2019, the US Department of Defense's 'Indo-Pacific Strategy Report' then broke with tradition by explicitly referring to Taiwan as a country.[84]

It is perhaps US actions rather than words that have contributed most to Chinese accusations that the US is challenging the cross-strait status quo. In April 2018, for instance, the US State Department confirmed that it had granted a licence to US defence companies allowing them to market submarine technology to Taiwan.[85] During Trump's presidency, the US has also approved a further four arms-sales packages – one in June 2017 worth US$1.4bn, one in September 2018 valued at US$330m, a third in April 2019 including F-16 fighter parts and training carrying a price tag of US$500m, and a fourth in June 2019 worth US$2bn including 108 *Abrams* tanks and US$220m in *Stinger* anti-aircraft missiles.[86] These sales have led to speculation that the US has returned to considering such requests annually, for the first time since that approach was dropped during the George W. Bush administration.[87]

In June 2018, the de facto US embassy in Taipei – the American Institute in Taiwan (AIT) – relocated to newly built premises worth US$250m. Although reports that a senior US administration official would attend the opening ceremony failed to materialise, Washington did confirm in April 2019 that it has been stationing active military personnel at the AIT since 2005 – a move which Beijing says violates the one China policy.[88] In March 2019, Taiwan's Minister of Foreign Affairs Joseph Wu and Director of the AIT Brent Christensen announced a new joint initiative, the Indo-Pacific Democratic Governance Consultations. These discussions, scheduled to be held for the first time in September 2019, are intended to provide 'a regular occasion for the United States and Taiwan to explore ways to increase their cooperation and pursue joint projects in the region', and will reportedly involve the participation of a senior US official.[89] In the highest-level exchange to date, Bolton in May 2019 met with his Taiwanese counterpart, David Lee, in the first publicly acknowledged contact between the heads of the US and Taiwanese national security councils since 1979.[90]

The Trump administration has also taken to publicising and regularising US transits of the Taiwan Strait. In May 2019, the *South China Morning Post* published data showing that US vessels had made 92 such transits between 2007 and April 2019. These peaked during the Obama administration, when transits reached double-digit figures in 2012, 2013, 2015 and 2016. Interestingly, however, the transits were never publicised and Beijing rarely objected publicly – except in 1996 and 2007, when the US sent aircraft-carrier battle groups through the strait.[91] This pattern has altered during the Trump administration, where transits are now routinely made public and conducted on a monthly basis in the name of demonstrating US commitment to a 'free and open Indo-Pacific'.[92] Other countries have followed Washington's lead and conducted transits of the Taiwan Strait, such as Australia (in September 2018),[93] France (in April 2019)[94] and Canada (in June 2019).[95]

Under pressure

Patrick Murphy, US deputy assistant secretary for East Asian and Pacific affairs, recently charged that Beijing has been 'busy' altering the cross-strait status quo.[96] Tsai has expressed similar sentiments, warning Beijing against unilaterally changing the status quo when two Chinese fighters jets crossed the Taiwan Strait's median line in March 2019 – the first purposeful encroachment of this kind in two decades.[97] However, Taipei, Beijing and Washington are all now challenging the cross-strait status quo. Although Taiwan remains unlikely to formally declare independence, its affinity with the mainland is clearly diminishing, while the Tsai administration is also increasingly emphasising Taiwan's 'sovereignty'. Beijing too remains unlikely to invade the island, except in the event of Taiwan declaring its independence. Nonetheless, it has stepped up its use of military force to threaten and coerce the island. Meanwhile, anti-China and pro-Taiwan sentiment are both rising in Washington, leading to the most openly supportive US policies towards the island seen since the height of the Cold War. These developments are all putting strains on the cross-strait status quo that has largely kept the peace across the Taiwan Strait. Shifts in the underlying balance of military power between China, Taiwan and the US are both facilitating this trend and potentially exacerbating it.

CHAPTER TWO

A complex balance of power

The balance of power between China, Taiwan and the United States has traditionally been thought of in straightforward military terms. As this chapter details, however, since the mid-1990s the distribution of military power between China and Taiwan has tilted decisively in Beijing's favour. Washington could once largely manage and manipulate that cross-strait balance due to the overwhelming preponderance of military power it enjoyed over China. However, the increasingly modern and capable People's Liberation Army (PLA) is developing the wherewithal to challenge the ability of the US to come to Taiwan's defence. This chapter assesses that the US will probably lose that ability altogether within the next decade. The growing array of economic incentives and coercive instruments that an increasingly assertive China is using to pressure Taiwan is exacerbating these shifts and making the balance between the three powers even more complex.

The cross-strait balance

For much of the modern history of this flashpoint, it was possible to refer accurately to a balance of military power between China and Taiwan. China's armed forces were significantly larger than those of Taiwan. When the US alliance with Taiwan formally ended on 1 January 1980, for instance, the IISS *Military Balance* recorded China's total armed forces at 4.36 million – significantly more than the 539,000 at Taiwan's disposal. But most of this quantitative advantage was concentrated in the mainland's larger land forces, which accounted for 3.6m (or over 80%) of China's total order of battle. China's navy and air force remained small and relatively weak. In terms of major surface combat ships, for example, Taiwan outnumbered the mainland 40 to 25 – meaning that Beijing lacked the power-projection capabilities needed to retake the island by force.[1]

Taiwan also enjoyed a qualitative military edge over China for much of the Cold War. Thanks to its alliance with the US, it had access to more sophisticated weaponry than did China; even when that strategic tie was downgraded as the chief casualty of Sino-American normalisation, Taiwan was still able to access US weaponry courtesy of the Taiwan Relations Act (TRA). Taipei simultaneously moved to diversify its arms suppliers to more than 20 other countries, with a view to reducing its dependence upon the US.[2]

In the early 1990s Taiwan also formally gave up the goal of reclaiming the mainland, meaning that it was able to downsize its disproportionately large army from approximately 240,000 personnel (out of an active force of 376,000) in 1997 to 88,000 (out of an active force of 163,000) in 2019, investing the savings into better equipping its navy and air force. Taiwan's geography supported this defensive mindset, further reinforcing its position in the cross-strait military balance. The island is protected on its east coast by imposing cliffs, while its west coast is lined with mud flats. There are few suitable areas to beach here and those which are conducive to amphibious landings can be defended relatively easily. Powerful winds blow down from Siberia during the winter months (December to February), while the weather is also unpredictable and highly inclement with an average of six tropical storms and typhoons annually between July and September, while strong, dangerous wave swells and tides are a feature of these waters. Given these natural constraints, PLA defence planners reportedly believe that there are only two windows – late March to late April and late September to late October – when a cross-strait military campaign could realistically be carried out.[3]

During the mid-1990s, however, the cross-strait military balance began to shift decisively in China's favour. Several factors contributed to this. The collapse of the Soviet Union in 1991 led to major Russian weapons systems subsequently becoming available for purchase by China because of Moscow's desperate need for hard currency. Moreover, the relative ease with which the US prevailed against Saddam Hussein's battle-hardened armed forces in the 1990–91 Gulf War shocked China's leaders and highlighted the need for serious military reform. The Clinton administration's dispatch of two aircraft-carrier battle groups to the Taiwan Strait during the 1995–96 crisis reinforced their anxieties. It not only confirmed the United States' continued commitment to Asia – a commitment that was being called into question after the Cold War[4] – but also deepened Beijing's resolve to find ways to resist external interventions of this kind in the future.

On the back of the remarkable economic growth that China enjoyed following Deng Xiaoping's historic 'Open Door' policy of the late 1970s, Beijing began to increase its defence expenditure significantly. While the official figure provided by Beijing in 1997 was US$9.7 billion, for instance, that year's edition of the IISS *Military Balance* put it at US$35bn. Taiwan's defence budget, by contrast, was US$11.6bn.[5] The picture today is dramatically different. According to the 2019 *Military Balance*,

China's defence expenditure has increased to US$168.2bn, making it the second largest in the world by a considerable margin.[6] Taiwan's defence expenditure, by contrast, stands at US$11bn – slightly less than two decades earlier.[7] To be sure, Tsai Ing-wen has pledged to reverse this downward trend, increasing the island's defence budget by 1.9% for 2018 and a further 5.6% for 2019.[8] Even with such increases, though, the gap between Taiwanese and Chinese defence expenditure will continue to grow, with significant ramifications for the cross-strait military balance.

The disparity is starkest for submarine capabilities. As of 2019, China has a total of 59 submarines in its arsenal. Ten of these are nuclear-powered, while the remaining 49 diesel-powered vessels are far quieter and thus harder to detect than the antiquated boats – based on 1950s-era technology – which constituted the bulk of its submarine force in the mid-1990s.[9] Taiwan, by contrast, has only four submarines. Two of these are Second World War-era boats, provided by the US, which can no longer fire torpedoes (although they can lay mines).[10] Taiwan's other two submarines are also diesel-powered, provided by the Netherlands during the 1980s. George W. Bush's administration approved the transfer of eight diesel-powered submarines to Taiwan as part of a large and controversial arms sale in April 2001, but these ultimately failed to materialise. By then, the US manufactured only nuclear-powered submarines and was unable to supply diesel-powered boats itself. European governments were unwilling to allow their own defence industries to supply Taiwan with submarines or submarine technology on behalf of the US for fear of provoking Beijing.[11]

Given this lack of international support, Tsai Ing-wen's government decided to launch an ambitious Indigenous Defense Submarine (IDS) programme. Its goal is to build domestically eight diesel-powered submarines and to have them operating within a decade. Four years of this will be spent designing the submarines, four years building them and the final two years in testing. In December 2016, the government awarded CSBC Corporation, a Taiwanese shipbuilder, a contract worth US$80m to design the submarines, and in October 2018, the Gibraltar-based defence contractor Gavron Ltd beat six foreign competitors (from the US, Europe, Japan and India) to win a contract worth US$1.6bn to oversee the design phase.[12] This progress notwithstanding, the IDS programme faces formidable obstacles. Taiwan has very little experience building major combat ships and none with submarines. The estimated cost of the project (US$5bn) will also eat up the bulk of the island's defence procurement budget, leaving little for the purchase of other much-needed weapons platforms.[13]

Similar disparities are evident between their air capabilities, where a substantial 'fighter gap' has opened up. For a time during the early 1990s, Taipei seemed willing and able to keep pace with China's burgeoning capabilities in this area. During this period, for instance, it was successful in purchasing 150 F-16 fighters from the US – albeit the less capable A/B variant of this aircraft – and 60 *Mirage* 2000 fighters from France, to add to the 130 indigenous *Ching-kuo* fighters which were commissioned in the late 1980s and entered service in the late 1990s. However, the increased Chinese air operations around Taiwan that are detailed later in this chapter are placing a considerable strain on this ageing force.

Meanwhile, the quality of aircraft and weapons systems operated by China's PLA Air Force (PLAAF) has improved exponentially. According to *The Military Balance 2019*, China has 2,413 combat-capable aircraft compared with Taiwan's 479.[14] Moreover, Taiwan's ageing fleet will increasingly face more modern and sophisticated Chinese aircraft, such as its first fifth-generation fighter (the J-20) and Russia's most advanced fighter (the Su-35).[15] Taipei had previously expressed interest in acquiring the F-35 Joint Strike Fighter (JSF) to offset this advantage and had some US congressional support for doing so. However, Washington would ultimately regard this as a bridge too far in terms of raising Beijing's ire, and is also concerned over the potential for technological 'leakage' from Taiwan to China. Consistent with that assessment, reports emerged in November 2018 that Taipei had decided to cease its JSF requests.[16] It opted instead to upgrade its existing F-16 fleet from A/B to F-16V *Viper* standard – the most advanced F-16 variant – while also requesting, in March 2019, to buy up to 66 F-16Vs from the US.[17] President Trump granted this request in August 2019, subject to congressional approval. However, this transfer will still only go some way toward closing the widening cross-strait fighter gap.

The disparity is equally stark for missiles. China currently targets approximately 1,200 short-range ballistic missiles (SRBMs), 400 land-attack cruise missiles (LACMs) and an unknown number of medium-range ballistic missiles (MRBMs) at the island. Taiwan's response since 2011, when these deployments began, has been slow for two reasons. Its own missile programme did not start until the late 1960s, and the island's first indigenously produced missiles did not enter service for another decade. Furthermore, Washington has traditionally exerted pressure upon Taipei to limit its development of weaponry to that of a defensive nature. While the distinction between 'offensive' and 'defensive' systems is often blurred, US policymakers have consistently regarded long-range missiles as falling into the former category. As the Chinese missile threat to the island has become more apparent, however, Washington from 2013 seems to have loosened this requirement. Hence, the island has begun producing longer-range missiles, with unconfirmed reports suggesting that one of these has a range of approximately 2,000 kilometres.[18] Nonetheless, the missile gap between China and Taiwan remains substantial.

Of course, there are limits to the usefulness of numerical disparities between opposing forces as indicators of comparative capability. Any assessment of the cross-strait balance ought to be considered in the context of actual conflict scenarios. It is certainly conceivable that Beijing's advantages on paper may not translate into performance on the battlefield due, for instance, to the PLA's inexperience in high-intensity combat.[19] Moreover, considering different categories of military capability in isolation is far from ideal. As Tim Huxley of the International Institute for Strategic Studies has recently observed:

> Military capability is complex, and buying new 'kit' does not provide countries with instant capabilities, as is often inferred. Other important elements of capability include appropriate doctrine, suitable training, inspiring leadership, high morale, vital logistic support (including defence-industrial capacity) … and a high level of operational integration between military branches and services. Besides, mastery of the cyber domain may be emerging as the *sine qua non* of military capability, potentially providing the capacity to take down an opponent's ability and will to fight even before a shot is fired.[20]

That said, Taiwan is currently struggling to maintain even the most basic elements of a fighting force. With an ageing and soon to be shrinking population, and given its growing unpopularity among younger Taiwanese, the Tsai administration was forced to abandon the island's long-standing conscription system – which Ma Ying-jeou had previously sought to phase out in 2011 – from 2018. These negative demographic trends will also inevitably impact upon the size of Taiwan's defence budget, as a smaller, older population generates lower government revenues and places a greater strain upon those which are raised.[21] As it moves to become an all-volunteer force, Taiwan's military is already struggling to meet recruitment numbers.[22] While military reforms in China are also leading to a streamlining of the PLA, with an active-duty force of 2,035,000 personnel, it is now more than ten times the size of Taiwan's.[23]

Some commentators maintain that the island's best and only hope is to respond to these imbalances by adopting a more explicitly asymmetric force structure and approach – the so-called 'Porcupine strategy.'[24] The primary aim of such an approach is to deter Beijing from initiating military action against the island in the first place, out of fear that the invading force would face a protracted and prohibitively costly operation. To be sure, asymmetry has long constituted a component of Taiwan's defence strategy. Moreover, Taipei's efforts to develop asymmetric capabilities have intensified over the past decade. Taiwan's navy, for instance, has developed a prototype for a fleet of stealthy, missile-equipped fast-attack vessels, which it hopes to have in service by 2021.

But Taiwanese legislators have questioned the tactical merits of this programme and it has become mired in the island's defence-budgetary problems, with the navy's allocation for the project trimmed in December 2018.[25] Moreover, advocates of the Porcupine posture have argued that such efforts do not go far enough and that effectively implementing such a strategy to counter the widening cross-strait military balance will require a far more extensive trading off of costly higher-end conventional platforms, such as fighter aircraft and submarines.[26] As the Taiwan-based analyst J. Michael Cole has argued,

despite improvements in recent years, the Taiwanese
military has yet to fully embrace the potential for an
asymmetrical response to the threat of an amphibious assault by China. Moreover, on the whole, Taiwan
remains committed to a traditional posture even
though the widening imbalance of power across the
strait is making that approach increasingly untenable. … As with military forces worldwide, resistance
to change and a lack of imagination has undermined
the willingness of Taiwanese military planners to fully
embrace recent scientific developments in the fields of
artificial intelligence (AI), ubiquitous remote-sensing
and automation.[27]

The US–China balance

Were China to invade Taiwan, it has long been assumed that
the island's armed forces would need to hold out for two to
four weeks to allow sufficient time for US assistance to arrive
from across the Pacific.[28] This assumes, of course, that the US
hadn't already been able to concentrate significant forces in
the Western Pacific during any sustained period of tension that
preceded outright hostilities. Up until relatively recently, there
has been little reason to question the ability of the US military to
provide that assistance under either scenario. The only uncertainties have concerned whether Washington would be willing
to offer such support. A recent study by the RAND Corporation,
for instance, estimates that US military superiority over China
at the time of the 1995–96 Taiwan Strait crisis was such that US
forces could have achieved air superiority within as little as
seven days of a conflict erupting, using less than a single air
wing of 72 fighters. The study judges that US military advantage in the maritime domain was similarly overwhelming.[29]

The course of the 1995–96 Taiwan Strait crisis significantly influenced Chinese strategic thinking, however, with profound ramifications for the Sino-American military balance. In the immediate aftermath of this crisis, Chinese strategists became increasingly focused upon developing what Western analysts and armed forces refer to as anti-access and area-denial (or A2/AD) capabilities. Anti-access capabilities are those which prevent an adversary entering an operational theatre to begin with, whereas area-denial capabilities contest an adversary's ability to move freely within that area. In Beijing's case, a primary motivation for pursuing A2/AD was to prevent US aircraft carriers from operating in China's maritime approaches as they had during the 1995–96 crisis.

A2/AD rests upon a 'family' of military capabilities consisting of anti-ship weapons (primarily cruise and ballistic missiles), the platforms needed to carry these (such as mobile land-based launchers, fast and stealthy short-range surface ships, quiet diesel-powered submarines, fighter aircraft and bombers) along with the reconnaissance, surveillance and target-acquisition technologies needed to support these.[30] Over the past two decades, China has taken significant leaps forward in each of these areas.

The centrepiece of China's A2/AD capabilities is its burgeoning missile programme. The range of China's missiles has increased markedly. Of particular relevance to a Taiwan contingency, the *Dong Feng* 21 (DF-21D) has an estimated range of 1,450–1,550 km. It has been dubbed the 'carrier killer', given that it was designed specifically to attack ships at sea. The *Dong Feng* 26 (DF-26) is a longer-range variant of the DF-21 prototype. It has an estimated range of 3,000–4,000 km. It is designed for attacks against both land and sea targets – including aircraft carriers – and can carry either conventional or nuclear warheads.[31]

The accuracy of China's missiles has also improved. The DF-21D, for instance, can reportedly strike within 20 metres or less of a target identified at its maximum range, while early estimates suggest that the DF-26 can strike within 150–450 m at its longer range.[32] The reconstitution of the Second Artillery Force as the People's Liberation Army Rocket Force (PLARF) in late 2015, and its elevation to the status of a full service of the PLA, further reinforces the importance that Beijing attaches to its growing missile capabilities. As Adam Ni and Bates Gill have written regarding this development, 'the establishment of the PLARF signals the increasing importance of conventional and nuclear missiles to PLA warfighting and deterrence capabilities. It also foreshadows continued, substantial investment in missile force modernization at both tactical and strategic levels in the years ahead.'[33]

US Air Force bases on Okinawa and Guam are especially vulnerable to China's growing missile capabilities. Indeed, another motivation for China developing A2/AD capabilities was to compensate for the weakness of its aircraft relative to the US by targeting the latter's while they were still on the ground. There are surprisingly few US air bases in this region – a problem unlikely to be resolved soon due to domestic opposition in allied countries to any increase in the US military presence. According to Oriana Mastro and Ian Easton, the relatively small number of US facilities in Asia are highly vulnerable due to a lack of adequate protection measures. Unlike Taiwan – which famously built an air base inside a hollowed-out mountain – Mastro and Easton report that four out of the eight US bases in Asia lack hardened aircraft shelters. This is partly for reasons of cost and partly also because China has only developed the capacity to strike accurately at these facilities with sufficient numbers of missiles within the last decade. They estimate, that the US would lose 70% of its aircraft based at the front-line air base in Kadena, Japan, during the opening salvos of a conflict over Taiwan. The same is true of another major facility – at Anderson Air Base on Guam – which is technically within range of the DF-26. Hence, through successfully executing an A2/AD approach, Beijing could ultimately stymie US intervention in a Taiwan scenario.[34]

China's ability to deny the US air superiority in a Taiwan contingency has also improved markedly since the 1995–96 crisis. At that time, the PLAAF and People's Liberation Army Navy (PLAN) operated antiquated second-generation fighter aircraft based upon 1950s-era Soviet technology. Today, these are being phased out and replaced with fourth-generation planes. Indeed, the PLAAF currently operates almost 800 fourth-generation fighters sourced either from Russia (such as its 52 Su-27, 73 Su-30 and 24 Su-35 fighters) or built indigenously (such as its 400-plus J-10, 225 J-11 and 60 J-16 fighter aircraft). These aircraft are comparable in performance to US fighters, such as the F-15 and the F-16. Moreover, China is developing the indigenously built J-20 and J-31 – currently the only stealth fighters in the world except for the F-22 and the F-35.[35]

These advances mean that the US would no longer be able to gain superiority with less than a single air wing and within a week of hostilities commencing, as the aforementioned RAND study estimated would have been the case at the time of the 1995–96 crisis. Instead, the same RAND study assesses that achieving air superiority within this time frame today would require between four and seven US fighter wings. This is significant because there are currently not sufficient US bases in theatre to accommodate that number of aircraft. According to RAND estimates, the number of aircraft required to achieve air superiority in a Taiwan scenario could be reduced to between 2.8 and 4.1 air wings if the time frame was also relaxed to within three weeks of hostilities commencing. Yet even that number of fighter aircraft would stretch current US basing capabilities to their very limit, while a three-week time frame also begins to test the two to four week period for which Taiwan's armed forces could likely hold out as they potentially awaited American reinforcements.[36]

Similar trends are apparent in the maritime domain. The PLAN is already larger than its US counterpart. The Pentagon in its May 2019 annual report to Congress on Chinese military power estimated that China has 335 combat ships now in service.[37] According to the RAND Corporation, approximately 70% of these are classified as 'modern' vessels when measured against contemporary standards of shipbuilding.[38] As of August 2019, by contrast, the US Navy had 291 deployable combat ships.[39] China's quantitative advantage is the product of a concerted effort, accelerated since 2015,[40] to improve both the quantity and the quality of China's surface-combatant force through the production of new cruisers, guided-missile destroyers, guided-missile frigates and corvettes. Potentially adding to Beijing's A2/AD capabilities, these new vessels are also being armed with anti-ship cruise missiles, including in some cases China's newest missile in this class – the YJ-18, with an estimated range of 537 km – and the supersonic YJ-12 anti-ship cruise missile.[41]

China has a considerable way to go before it can match some elements of the US surface fleet. Aircraft carriers serve as a case in point. China already has a medium-sized, ex-Soviet carrier in service – the *Liaoning* – and a second indigenously built carrier undergoing sea trials. There are also reports of a third and possibly even a fourth – each likely larger and more capable – carrier under construction.[42] This remains a considerable distance behind the US, which currently operates 11 strike groups, each centred around a large, nuclear-powered aircraft carrier. However, what role these or China's nascent carrier fleet would ultimately play in a Taiwan contingency is far from certain, especially given Beijing's growing A2/AD capabilities and the longer-range, anti-ship missiles that the US is currently developing in response. As Lyle Goldstein, a professor at the US Naval War College, has observed,

> one needs to keep in mind that evolving naval warfare is almost certain to be inhospitable to *any* surface ships, American or Chinese. The projected future environment, therefore, where submarines, missiles and, to a lesser extent, aircraft rule the waves, seems quite unlikely to yield up major surface engagements.[43]

China is also gaining ground as far as the undersea balance is concerned, although this is an area where US submarines look set to retain a qualitative edge for at least the next decade. US submarines remain quicker and quieter than their Chinese counterparts. They are equipped with more powerful sonar and carry superior weaponry.[44] Analysts have traditionally regarded anti-submarine warfare as an area of weakness for China. At the same time, however, China's newer *Song*- and *Yuan*-class conventional submarines are equipped with advanced anti-ship cruise missiles, such as the YJ-18, thus adding further to its A2/AD capabilities.[45] These smaller diesel-powered submarines are also better placed to negotiate the shallow waters of the Taiwan Strait, relative to their much larger, nuclear-powered American counterparts. A far more significant challenge for Washington as far as US submarine capabilities in a Taiwan contingency are concerned, however, is the widening quantitative gap that is opening up between the US and China. Based upon current production and acquisition trends, for instance, China could have as many as 100 submarines by the early 2030s, while the US, by contrast, could have as few as 41 attack submarines at its disposal.[46]

China is also gaining ground in surveillance and precision-guided technologies, even though this has traditionally been, and remains, an area of real US strength due to the sophisticated architecture consisting of satellites, listening posts and radar stations, and military platforms (including maritime-patrol aircraft, acoustic monitoring ships, nuclear-powered submarines and drones) whose operation US practitioners have perfected over several decades of experience. China had virtually no such capability to speak of at the time of the 1995–96 Taiwan Strait crisis. During the period since, it has developed a sophisticated network of fixed sonar arrays deep in the so-called 'near seas' surrounding China, it has deployed powerful over-the-horizon radar with an estimated range of 2,000 km, and it has put military imaging satellites of progressively better quality into space. As the Pentagon's 2018 report to Congress on Chinese military and security developments observes, the

> PLAN recognizes that long-range [anti-ship cruise missiles] require a robust, over-the-horizon targeting capability to realize their full potential. China is investing in reconnaissance, surveillance, command, control and communications systems at the strategic, operational and tactical levels to provide high-fidelity targeting information to surface and subsurface launch platforms.[47]

There remain considerable uncertainties when assessing the US–China military balance, including cyber capabilities, combat experience, leadership, and morale and societal support for the armed forces. One related uncertainty concerns the necessary level of secrecy on both sides. As Andrew Erickson, a US analyst of Chinese military affairs, correctly notes, 'a truly comprehensive net assessment requires considering all elements of a complex, multivariate force-on-force campaign. This includes information currently unavailable from open sources. While scholarship and public debate demand unclassified analysis, researchers should acknowledge its limitations explicitly.'[48] Added to this is the uncertain impact of technological advances and breakthroughs. The US, for instance, is currently developing directed-energy and long-range hypersonic-railgun technologies, as well as large quantities of drones and unmanned surface vessels to compensate for its declining ship numbers and to counter China's increasingly potent A2/AD capabilities.[49] Following the expiry on 1 February 2019 of the 1987 Intermediate-Range Nuclear Forces Treaty, then-acting US Secretary of Defense Mark Esper indicated in August 2019 his desire to base intermediate-range missiles in Asia, again in direct response to China's burgeoning intermediate-range missile arsenal.[50] US forces are also thought to receive better training than their Chinese counterparts – even though the latter are seeking to introduce greater levels of realism into this aspect of their preparedness. But it remains unclear whether decades of military action in the Middle East would provide an advantage to US forces in a high-intensity conflict with China over Taiwan.

These 'known unknowns' notwithstanding, the strategic geography of this flashpoint overwhelmingly favours China. Taiwan is approximately 11,000 km from the continental United States. By contrast, it is a mere 160 km from mainland China at its closest point. Consistent with this, China has almost 40 air bases within an unrefuelled-fighter range of approximately 800 km from the island. The US has only one (Kadena Air Base) within that range, and just three bases within 1,500 km.[51] This geographic advantage, coupled with China's growing A2/AD capabilities, means that the US would still be able to come to Taiwan's defence, but at considerably greater cost and risk than in the 1995–96 crisis. But, should current trends in the US–China military balance continue along their present trajectory, it will most likely have lost that capacity by 2030.

An expanding toolbox

As China's economic and military weight increases, so too does the range of coercive instruments at its disposal. Military coercion is a particularly prevalent feature of Beijing's approach towards Taiwan. This was not always the case. Following the use of high-profile military exercises in the lead-up to the island's 1996 presidential election, for instance, Beijing appeared to de-emphasise the use of military coercion, fearing that this had provoked a strong US response, hardened the resolve of Taiwan's inhabitants and heightened regional fears of an emerging 'China threat'. In the run-up to Taiwan's March 2000 presidential election China's leaders instead relied largely upon bellicose rhetoric: then Chinese premier Zhu Rongji publicly warned the island's inhabitants against voting for Democratic Progressive Party (DPP) candidate Chen Shui-bian: 'Let me advise all these people in Taiwan, do not act on impulse … Otherwise, I'm afraid you won't get another opportunity to regret.'[52] Once again, however, the electorate delivered precisely the outcome that Beijing had – apparently with counterproductive effect – warned against, with Chen winning the presidency after securing 39% of the vote in a bitter three-way race involving the popular independent candidate James Soong (36.8%) and Kuomintang (KMT) candidate Lien Chan (23.1%).

Beijing returned to military coercion as a tactic to pressure Taiwan following Tsai's election. The PLA responded to her victory by conducting live-fire drills in the southeastern city of Xiamen, directly opposite Taiwan and close to the offshore island of Kinmen (formerly Quemoy) which was a focal point of the first and second Taiwan Strait crises of the 1950s.[53] In the days before Tsai's inauguration in May 2016, the PLA staged another large-scale exercise in Xiamen which included simulated amphibious operations and helicopter assaults.[54] From November 2016, the PLAAF then began undertaking so-called 'island encirclement patrols' around Taiwan.[55] These patrols are often performed by H-6 bombers, in tandem with various combinations of Su-30, J-10 and J-11 fighters and other support aircraft. On occasion, such as in April 2018, these patrols have occurred several days in a row. Chinese media commentary suggests that their purpose is to deter separatist sentiment on the island.[56] The *Liaoning* has also transited through the Taiwan Strait with greater frequency, although on each occasion thus far it has remained on the Chinese side of the median line in this narrow body of water.[57]

Beijing has also been employing a growing array of non-military instruments and techniques designed to deter the island's drift from the mainland and to incentivise reunification. Indeed, since at least the mid-1970s, Taiwan's leaders have increasingly expressed anxiety over the economic threat from China as much as, if not more than, the military one.[58] They have feared that cross-strait trade and financial ties will eventually draw the island inexorably into the mainland's embrace. For this reason, Taiwan banned investment on the mainland until the early 1990s. Since the lifting of that ban, China has become Taiwan's biggest destination for investment, although this has declined steadily in recent years. In 2017, for instance, Taiwanese businesses invested US$8.7bn on the mainland, a 30% drop from 2011 when investment levels were at their highest.[59] But China remains Taiwan's leading export destination, accounting for approximately 40% of the island's exports (a figure including the approximately 12.5% of exports sent to Hong Kong). Around 80% of these exports consist of intermediary goods assembled on the mainland and then either sold there or exported to third countries.[60]

Taipei's worst fears appeared to materialise in February 2018, when China's Taiwan Affairs Office issued a set of '31 Measures' offering greater opportunities for Taiwanese on the mainland. Reportedly the product of extensive consultations within both the Chinese government and the Communist Party, this new suite of policies was consistent with Xi's October 2017 address to the 19th Party Congress, in which he pledged to 'share the development opportunities on the mainland with our Taiwanese compatriots first' and to 'expand cross-straits economic and cultural exchanges and cooperation for mutual benefits'.[61] Twelve of the new measures relate to Taiwanese businesses, offering them various tax breaks and subsidies, the opportunity to bid with Chinese counterparts for infrastructure-development projects and even the chance to become involved in China's ambitious Belt and Road Initiative (BRI). The remaining 19 measures are targeted at individuals, providing them with greater opportunity to live, work, study and start businesses on the mainland. Taipei regards the 31 Measures with a great deal of suspicion, not least because they bypass Taiwan's government by giving businesses and citizens the opportunity to deal directly with China. The Taiwanese government sees the policy as an attempt to undermine the island's economy by enticing capital and young talent away from Taiwan, thus compounding the brain drain caused by the hundreds of thousands of Taiwanese who have left the island to live and work on the mainland. Of Taiwan's working-age population of 11m, for example, official government statistics record 720,000 as having left the island for work, with over half of these venturing to the mainland. The unofficial figure is likely even higher.[62]

Tsai's government is striving to lessen Taiwan's economic vulnerability to the mainland. Indeed, one of the primary reasons for her landslide victory in 2016 was growing popular anxiety that the KMT government of Ma Ying-jeou had drifted too close to Beijing, both economically and politically. Seeking to address these fears, Tsai's signature foreign-policy initiative is the 'New Southbound Policy' (NSP). The NSP aims to expand and diversify the island's economic linkages with the ten countries of Southeast Asia, six South Asian countries (Bangladesh, Bhutan, India, Nepal, Pakistan and Sri Lanka), and Australia and New Zealand. Tsai's predecessors – Lee Teng-hui and Chen – introduced similar initiatives, with limited success. In Lee's case, the 1997–98 Asian financial crisis intervened; for both Lee and Chen, the pull of the mainland economy also ultimately proved too strong. Tsai's scheme is more ambitious than these earlier efforts, however, because it also envisages deepening people-to-people links with NSP target countries. In this way, it aims to circumvent the challenges caused by Taiwan's lack of formal diplomatic status by engaging at the interpersonal level, with a view to strengthening the island's regional integration over the medium to longer term.[63]

Beijing has an array of other coercive instruments that it employs both to curb Taiwanese efforts to chart a more independent path and to punish those who support such attempts. One enduring Chinese tactic has been to limit Taipei's international space. Beijing has ensured that Taiwan is excluded from most major multilateral arrangements. In a dramatic example of this approach, Taiwanese delegates at a May 2017 gathering of the Kimberley process – an intergovernmental meeting set up in 2000 to prevent the trade in 'conflict diamonds' – were forced to leave after Chinese delegates objected to their presence, shouting down the Australian chair of the meeting as he was attempting to introduce his country's foreign minister,

Julie Bishop, and a group performing an indigenous welcome ceremony.[64] Similarly, while Taiwan from 2009–16 was granted observer status in the World Health Assembly (WHA) – the premier meeting of the World Health Organization (WHO) – Taipei has not received a WHA invitation since 2017. This is reportedly due to Chinese pressure. Beijing's position is that Taiwan had only been invited to observe earlier gatherings because it had accepted the 'one China' policy.[65]

Beijing's efforts to entice countries who formally recognise Taiwan to switch diplomatic allegiance to China have also intensified. To be sure, most countries moved to formally recognise Beijing in 1971 after Taiwan lost the Chinese seat at the United Nations. Yet even during the 1990s, more than 30 countries still recognised Taiwan. That number has since shrunk to 17: five countries have switched allegiance to the People's Republic of China (PRC) since Tsai's election alone – Panama; São Tomé and Príncipe; the Dominican Republic; Burkina Faso; and, most recently, El Salvador in August 2018.[66] The following month, speculation began to intensify that the Vatican would also move to formally recognise China, after signing a provisional agreement with Beijing that would allow the Holy See to provide input into the appointment of bishops on the mainland. Formal diplomatic ties between Beijing and the Holy See were originally severed in 1951.[67] Of the remaining governments which recognise Taipei, most are small, poor countries from Central America and the South Pacific – such as Guatemala, Nauru, Kiribati and Paraguay. Their small size and impoverished status render these countries susceptible to Chinese pressure in the form of financial inducements.

China is also actively pressuring foreign companies into not recognising the island. In a move described by Trump administration officials as 'Orwellian nonsense',[68] Beijing in April 2018 contacted 44 major international airlines and demanded that they stop referring to Taiwan as an independent country. Reflecting the importance of the Chinese market to their operations, all 44 carriers complied.[69] In a similarly assertive episode targeting the aviation sector, Beijing in January 2018 commenced four new flight routes close to the Taiwan Strait's median line. One of these routes flew within 7.8 km of the line, violating a deal made between Beijing and Taipei in 2015 which agreed that Chinese flights would not fly within 18.9 km of the median line. J. Michael Cole, a leading commentator on cross-strait relations, argues that the revocation of this agreement was designed to call into question Tsai's ability to defend the island and to undermine Taiwan's sovereignty claim.[70]

Beijing's multifaceted political-influence operations have also gained increased international attention in recent years. Trump has publicly accused Beijing of interfering in the November 2018 mid-term elections.[71] In Australia, Chinese attempts to intimidate members of that country's 1.2m-strong ethnic-Chinese diaspora, to influence public debate and to manipulate high-ranking politicians through political donations have become a subject of intense debate, and led the Australian government to introduce new legislation against foreign influence and foreign interference in June 2018.[72]

Taiwan is more experienced than most countries when it comes to exposure to these kinds of coercive methods. Indeed, the DPP's defeat in the November 2018 local elections has been seen in this light. While most analysts concur that the results can be explained by domestic factors, there is widespread speculation that a concerted anti-Tsai campaign orchestrated by Beijing on social-media platforms had a strong bearing upon this election result.[73] In December 2018, for instance, six US senators wrote a letter to the secretary of state, the secretary of the treasury, and the directors of National Intelligence and the FBI demanding that this speculation 'be pursued with seriousness and urgency'.[74] Taiwanese share these concerns: in a July 2019 Election Study Center poll, for instance, 65.7% of respondents agreed that 'disinformation could severely undermine Taiwan's democratic development'.[75]

Danger of escalation

The complex balance of power underpinning the China–Taiwan–US triangle is shifting, and increasing the prospect of military escalation. As the military imbalance between Taiwan and the mainland grows, and as China's ability to deny the US access to this theatre continues to improve, Beijing's incentives for resolving this dispute through the use of force will only increase. Moreover, as China's power grows, its range of options for addressing the 'Taiwan problem' is also expanding. That said, Beijing remains highly inexperienced at employing many of the new instruments now at its disposal. This inexperience, in turn, heightens the prospects for mishandling, miscalculation and misperception on all sides.

CHAPTER THREE

Tipping points

Almost two decades ago, the journalist Malcolm Gladwell published *The Tipping Point: How Little Things Can Make a Big Difference*.[1] Gladwell borrowed the concept of the 'tipping point' from epidemiology: it is that critical juncture at which an epidemic explodes. Gladwell was less concerned with where the tipping point was in relation to the trends he studied and more with the process of *how* that tipping point was arrived at. This chapter considers four possible pathways along which the Taiwan flashpoint might reach its tipping point and erupt into full-blown conflict: an 'accidental' crossing of Beijing's 'red lines'; an inadvertent military clash or miscalculation; Taiwan's return to 'proxy' status in a new Sino-American cold war; or the sudden emergence of military-technical incentives for escalation.

Red lines

Beijing has drawn numerous red lines in relation to Taiwan. In October 2017, for instance, Chinese Ambassador to the United States Cui Tiankai wrote formally to the US Congress to express his country's 'grave concern' regarding several pieces of new legislation, including the Taiwan Travel Act, and to threaten 'severe consequences' if these were passed. In Cui's words, these 'provocations against China's sovereignty, national unity and security interests … have crossed the "red line" on the stability of the China–US relationship'.[2] The hawkish Chinese newspaper *Global Times* in April 2018 characterised a live-fire military drill conducted by the People's Liberation Army (PLA) in the Taiwan Strait as 'draw[ing] a red line to the US and Taiwan'.[3] And in June 2018, when Beijing implored the Trump administration not to send a senior official to the opening of the new American Institute in Taiwan (AIT) compound in Taipei, an unnamed US official reportedly accused the Chinese of 'setting new red lines'.[4]

Since at least the early 2000s, Beijing has consistently characterised Taiwan as a 'core Chinese interest' that it would use military force to defend. Yet despite the obvious import of this issue to China's leaders, exactly where their red lines in relation to Taiwan lie remains far from clear. Indeed, just as the US has historically pursued a policy of 'strategic ambiguity' towards Taiwan, Beijing seems to see similar advantage in maintaining a level of obfuscation on the subject. As Scott Kastner, a US scholar of cross-strait relations, has observed, 'the PRC has clear incentives to overstate its resolve (meaning, in essence, to understate its expected costs of war), so as to convince Taiwan's leadership that its redline lies farther left (i.e. farther from independence and closer to unification) than might truly be the case … Indeed, the redlines that Beijing communicates in practice can themselves be ambiguous.'[5]

It is indeed hard to believe that Beijing would initiate potentially devastating military conflict in response to the attendance of a senior US official at an event or in retaliation against a piece of legislation. As such, the best available indicator for where Beijing's 'red lines' actually lie regarding Taiwan is contained in the 2005 Anti-Secession Law (ASL). Article 8 of the ASL states:

> In the event that the 'Taiwan independence' secession-ist forces should act under any name or by any means to cause the fact of Taiwan's secession from China, or that major incidents entailing Taiwan's secession from China should occur, or that possibilities for a peaceful reunification should be completely exhausted, the state shall employ non-peaceful means and other necessary measures to protect China's sovereignty and territorial integrity.[6]

A formal Taiwanese declaration of independence would very likely trigger a military response from China. Taiwanese public opinion has thus tended to reflect a high level of pragmatism in clear recognition of this risk. According to a 2013 poll canvassing a range of potential pathways to Taiwanese independence, for instance, 81.5% of respondents agreed with the statement 'if China recognizes Taiwan's independence, Taiwan should declare independence'. By contrast, only 38.8% of respondents agreed that Taiwan should declare independence if this risked a Chinese attack on the island.[7] A similar pragmatism is evident in the approach that successive Taiwanese presidential candidates have taken, including Chen Shui-bian, who in 2000 made a campaign commitment to pursue a 'new middle way' between Taiwan and the mainland; Ma Ying-jeou, who early in his 2008 presidential campaign called for maintenance of the status quo; and Tsai Ing-wen when she adopted a more moderate version of the Democratic Progressive Party's (DPP) pro-independence stance whilst on the campaign trail.[8]

As long as the Chinese military threat remains and intensifies, this deeply ingrained sense of pragmatism seems unlikely to change. As the political scientist Steve Tsang has observed,

> In Taiwan, whatever the personal preference of … any future leader holding the office of state president, he/she will not intentionally announce a policy that will immediately cause China to attack Taiwan. Given the centrality of China's reactions to a formal declaration of independence by Taiwan, no president in Taiwan would take such a step. Although public opinion in Taiwan continues to support governmental attempts to assert Taiwan's sense of identity and its existing membership in the international community, it should not be equated with favouring or provoking a war with China.[9]

What Beijing regards as the complete exhaustion of possibilities for peaceful reunification, and how patient China's leaders are willing to be on this point, is far less clear. There is much speculation, for instance, as to whether Xi has a timeline for resolving the 'Taiwan problem' and, if so, what deadline he has in mind. As noted in Chapter One, some commentators maintain that Xi could make a move for Taiwan as early as 2021, to coincide with the centenary of the founding of the Chinese Communist Party (CCP). Others are of the view that he will be content to wait until the centenary of the establishment of the People's Republic of China (PRC) in 2049 to see this issue settled by a successor. There is also ongoing debate within China – between a 'patient' and an 'impatient' school of thinking – regarding the timelines for Taiwan's reunification.

Where Beijing's red lines regarding Taiwan lie at any given time is heavily contingent upon domestic political dynamics on the mainland. There is significant debate among China analysts at present as to the security of Xi's position as leader. Many commentators, for instance, suggest that Xi is China's strongest leader since Mao, pointing in particular to the decision of the March 2018 National People's Congress to remove the traditional two-term limit on the presidency and essentially to allow Xi to remain China's leader for life.[10] Others, such as Harvard University's William Overholt, argue that Xi's position is far more precarious than this dominant narrative suggests, due primarily to discontent stemming from his brutal anti-corruption campaign and a slowing Chinese economy. In Overholt's view,

> Xi does not have the power to unilaterally implement his agenda or to remain in power indefinitely. His repression of opponents does not prove his invincibility; it reflects his vulnerability. His many titles reflect insecurity … Xi is vulnerable. He disappears from the media for days. An adulatory movie is suddenly curtailed. Portraits are suddenly removed. His bodyguards are suddenly changed.[11]

The security of Xi's grip on power has dramatic ramifications for any timelines he might have in mind regarding Taiwan's reunification. An all-powerful leader might well have the luxury of biding their time. A beleaguered president, however, simply could not afford to be seen as weak in the eyes of the Chinese people, especially when it comes to a highly sensitive and important issue like Taiwan. Respect for the CCP has declined markedly in recent years, both among policy elites and, more generally, throughout society. Xi's 'China Dream' is a direct response to this, and to the existential threat it potentially poses to the party. Xi clearly wants to lift the Party's image by raising the living standards and quality of life of all Chinese citizens. In large part, however, he is seeking to win support for this vision by appealing to China's history of humiliation and the need to never again be subjected to such treatment. Having set such expectations, Xi cannot thus credibly give ground on Taiwan without risking widespread criticism – particularly among Chinese 'netizens' – that his position is similar to the submissive stances of his nineteenth-century predecessors who allowed foreign concessions into Shanghai and who surrendered Hong Kong to the British.[12]

The ambiguity of Beijing's red lines regarding Taiwan is compounded further by the fact that they can also shift in response to domestic political developments within China itself. This means that there is considerable potential for miscalculation. As Kastner suggests, conflict might break out 'because there is some uncertainty regarding the precise location of Beijing's redlines, and it can be hard for Beijing to credibly communicate the true location of those redlines. As such, a revisionist Taiwan could trigger a military conflict by unintentionally crossing a Chinese redline.'[13] To be sure, Beijing and Taipei have historically relied upon the use of diplomatic back channels to clarify their respective positions and to avoid such miscalculations, even during periods when formal communication across the Taiwan Strait has ostensibly been frozen.[14] Yet informal channels have their limits, which can become readily apparent in the heat of a major strategic crisis.

Inadvertent escalation

As Asia's skies and strategic waterways become more crowded and contested, the potential for an inadvertent clash between military ships or aircraft is also rising. Such episodes are relatively frequent in the region. In April 2001, for instance, a collision between a Chinese fighter and a US EP-3 surveillance aircraft over the waters of the South China Sea sparked an international crisis.[15] Drawing comparisons with that earlier clash, a US warship (USS *Decatur*) and a Chinese destroyer (*Lanzhou*) came within approximately 40 metres of each other in September 2018. Commentators speculated that, had they clashed, the situation could quickly have escalated into a larger Sino-American conflict, given heightened tensions between Washington and Beijing.[16] Similar incidents have occurred in the adjacent East China Sea: in early 2013, for example, a Chinese vessel locked its fire-control radar – the step immediately preceding the potential firing of a weapon – onto a Japanese destroyer.[17]

The scope for serious mishap over the Taiwan flashpoint was demonstrated in July 2016 when a Taiwanese Navy corvette, docked at Zuoying naval base in the southern Taiwanese port of Kaohsiung, accidentally fired a live missile during a training exercise. The missile flew for two minutes toward the Penghu Islands – towards the mainland – before colliding with a Taiwanese fishing boat, killing its captain and injuring three of its crew. Ultimately, the anti-ship missile – which had a range of approximately 300 kilometres – did not cross the Taiwan Strait's tacitly understood median line. Subsequent investigations revealed the misfiring to be the product of human error – the corvette's missile-control system was set to 'combat mode' rather than 'training mode' – and led to the conviction of three Taiwanese Navy personnel for negligence.[18]

It is possible to envision a range of scenarios in which an inadvertent clash could occur between aircraft operating near Taiwan. In March 2019, for instance, two Chinese J-11 fighters crossed the median line. This was the first time that Chinese aircraft had purposefully done so in two decades, leading Taipei to scramble five F-16 fighters in response. A ten-minute stand-off ensued before the Chinese aircraft left the area. Following this incident, Tsai pledged that further encroachments across the median line would be subject to 'forceful expulsion'.[19]

As Chinese encirclement patrols have increased around the island, Taiwan has also begun scrambling aircraft to monitor these flights.[20] These patrols have apparently been undertaken at a distance of approximately 30 km, in an attempt to minimise the risk of a collision. However, recent reports suggesting that a Taiwanese fighter mistakenly fired a self-defence weapon (an infrared decoy projectile) in an unspecified encounter with a PLA aircraft,[21] coupled with the March 2019 stand-off, raises the chances of an inadvertent clash. This might involve two military aircraft colliding, or one aircraft switching its radar from 'search mode' to 'lock-on' mode, even when operating at a safe distance.[22] The likelihood of a collision between military and civilian aircraft has also grown following Beijing's introduction of new commercial flight routes close to the median line in January 2018, absent any prior consultation with Taipei.[23]

If such a clash occurred, the chances of escalation would be considerable. The military analyst Kenneth W. Allen, for instance, outlines a scenario where a Chinese military aircraft operating near the median line crashes due to pilot error or mechanical failure while close to Taiwanese military aircraft. The immediate response in such a scenario would be for Chinese ground controllers to dispatch search-and-rescue ships and aircraft to the area. However, because it could not be certain that the crash wasn't the result of a deliberate provocation, Beijing would also likely initiate combat patrols in the vicinity. The same is true in reverse. Taipei could also not afford to discount the possibility that the incident was the beginning of a larger operation, meaning that its armed forces would be put on high alert. This, in turn, would prompt a similar response from Beijing, who would put its armed forces on alert and who would also deploy additional aircraft near or over the Taiwan Strait.[24]

This same potential for rapid military escalation is present at sea. The risk of an accidental clash was highlighted in July 2019, when an unidentified People's Liberation Army Navy (PLAN) vessel mysteriously collided at night with a Taiwanese cargo ship near Kinmen Island.[25] In March 2018, Taipei sent naval ships and military aircraft to shadow a Chinese carrier battle group centred around the *Liaoning* as it transited through the Taiwan Strait.[26] The US naval analyst Bernard Cole has developed a detailed hypothetical scenario in which escalation could occur from an inadvertent clash between Chinese and Taiwanese vessels operating in close proximity. In Cole's scenario, Beijing calls for Taipei to engage in reunification talks with the mainland and issues an edict that any commercial shipping bound for Taiwan must first report to a Chinese port – in Wenzhou, Fuzhou or Xiamen, for instance – to obtain prior approval. Beijing sends military ships to enforce this order. Taiwan predictably responds by deploying its own naval vessels to ensure that merchant shipping to the island is not interrupted. In Cole's scenario, however, the situation quickly escalates when a Chinese submarine sinks a Taiwanese frigate, drawing in the US.[27]

Chinese military pundits have recently suggested that Beijing might sink a US aircraft carrier while it is transiting the Taiwan Strait. They contend that a casualty-averse US would vacate Asia altogether in the wake of such a heavy blow. Such an outcome is highly unlikely, however, given that the resultant loss of thousands of US lives would more likely spark a massive military response from Washington.[28] Sinking an aircraft carrier is also no easy task given the robustness of their design and composition.[29] Yet although no rational Chinese leader would intentionally take such a perilous course, it is still conceivable that such an outcome could arise inadvertently. As detailed in Chapter One, during the 1995–96 crisis in the Taiwan Strait, for instance, Beijing fired ballistic missiles that splashed down in sea lanes adjacent to Taiwan's two main seaports – in Kaohsiung and Keelung – with a view to intimidating the island's inhabitants.[30] In a variation on this approach, it is plausible that during a future Taiwan Strait crisis, Beijing might fire close to a transiting US carrier group to signal both its displeasure and its resolve. While it may have absolutely no intention of doing so, a technical error could conceivably lead to this 'shot across the bow' accidentally striking a US vessel. As the US scholar Avery Goldstein has observed, 'even a fully operational ASBM [anti-ship ballistic missile] capability that performs to specifications will have a margin of error determined not only by the warhead's terminal guidance, but also by the time that passes between tracking, targeting, launching, and impact'.[31]

Some commentators contend that the threat of major conflict stemming from an inadvertent act are overblown. They point to the experience of the Cold War, during which there were innumerable episodes at the local or tactical level which ultimately didn't spiral out of control. As the former US naval officer Steven Stashwick argues,

> despite explicit mutual, strategic and existential antagonism between the US and USSR, none of the *hundreds* of maritime incidents that occurred over the four decades of the Cold War escalated into anything beyond a short diplomatic crisis. It is possible that they avoided a nuclear spiral in these incidents through diligent diplomacy and luck. But, more likely, it suggests that this type of maritime incident is insufficient on its own to lead to the worst-case scenarios envisioned.[32]

Yet such optimistic assessments underestimate the deep-seated nationalisms which are a general feature of Northeast Asia's security politics and the Taiwan flashpoint in particular. As Chang goes on to observe, 'in China the Taiwan issue is seen through the prism of morality, the future of the Chinese state and national honor, and growing resentment against Taiwan's incremental approach to asserting independence'.[33] Were Taiwan's misfiring of an anti-ship missile to have occurred exactly five years later in the nationalistically charged atmosphere of the CCP's centenary celebrations, for instance, and were that missile to cross the median line and strike a Chinese fishing vessel or, worse still, a military ship, the chances of an escalatory response from Beijing would be considerable.

Elsewhere in Asia, efforts are being made to reduce the risk of such incidents and to manage its escalation should one occur. In April 2014, for example, 21 nations meeting under the auspices of the Western Pacific Naval Symposium agreed to a set of (albeit non-binding) rules for avoiding inadvertent maritime clashes known as the Code for Unplanned Encounters at Sea (CUES).[34] In June 2018, after a decade of negotiations, China and Japan launched a new 'communication mechanism' designed to avoid accidental clashes both in the air and at sea.[35] And in September 2018, the two Koreas agreed to introduce a range of new 'risk reduction' measures, including the establishment of a no-fly zone along their shared border, a so-called 'maritime peace zone' in the Yellow Sea, a halt to artillery and other military exercises in the demilitarised zone (DMZ) separating the two countries, and the removal of several guard posts along the DMZ.[36] In January of the same year, Pyongyang and Seoul also reactivated a hotline in the village of Panmunjom – where the July 1953 Korean War armistice was signed – which North Korean leader Kim Jong-un and South Korean President

Moon Jae-in then used to speak to each other before their historic summit in April 2018.[37]

China and Taiwan have no comparable arrangements in place. To be sure, China and Taiwan did launch a new hotline for communication between senior officials from Taiwan's Mainland Affairs Council and the mainland's Taiwan Affairs Office in December 2015. This initiative was a key outcome of the previous month's Singapore summit, when Xi became the first PRC leader to meet with his Taiwanese counterpart, Ma Ying-jeou, since the Chinese Civil War.[38] The hotline was used on at least four occasions in early 2016 but has since gone dead, with the Chinese side reportedly not answering since Tsai's inauguration.[39] This silent treatment is dangerous, however, because it heightens the prospects for escalation occurring in the aftermath of an inadvertent clash of the kind described above. As Kenneth Allen concludes,

> if there is no hotline between the two sides … and neither Taipei nor Beijing takes public responsibility for the event, this activity could be misinterpreted by the other side as a provocation, leading to rapid escalation … This situation could rapidly get out of control unless both sides communicate with each other to determine the exact cause of the accident and agree to de-escalate the situation.[40]

A new cold war?

Some commentators describe deepening strategic competition between China and the US as a new cold war. As with the original struggle between the US and the Soviet Union, they see this new iteration as a contest with several inter-related dimensions. They regard Sino-American competition as exhibiting some of the characteristics of traditional great-power politics, particularly those which are manifest when an aspiring hegemon starts to challenge a preponderant power. More importantly, however, as in the case of the original cold war they point to a deep ideological divergence in values between the ruling regimes of these two powers. They identify an economic angle, as epitomised by the so-called 'trade war'. Relatedly, this commentary also argues that the new Sino-American cold war has a technological aspect, as exemplified by the prevalence of illicit Chinese cyber intrusions into US business networks and Western societies more broadly.[41]

In October 2018, US Vice President Mike Pence delivered a combative speech at the Hudson Institute in Washington DC. Some commentators likened it to British prime minister Winston Churchill's famous 'Iron Curtain' address of March 1946, which marked the symbolic beginning of the original Cold War.[42] Significantly, Pence's address gave prominence to Taiwan, stating that the US 'will always believe Taiwan's embrace of democracy shows a better path for all the Chinese people'.[43] Quite what a new Sino-American cold war would mean for Taiwan is unclear. Some commentators worry that the island could be severely buffeted by the winds of a fully blown US–China trade war. China and the US are the island's two leading trading partners, Taiwan is a key link in supply chains running to the US through China, while some Chinese exports to the US are produced by major Taiwanese companies based on the mainland.[44] Conversely, others see advantages for Taiwan, believing that the island's strategic value to the US will increase exponentially as Sino-US competition intensifies. From this perspective, Taipei can expect increasingly robust and enthusiastic support from Washington.[45] Indeed, as Chapter One of this book argues, a strong case can be made that this is already happening.

As welcome as such support undoubtedly seems for Taipei, it does not come without risk. As in the original Cold War, should the island's perceived strategic significance in the wider US–China contest increase, the prospects for military escalation from this flashpoint will almost certainly grow. Throughout the Cold War, Washington was attuned to the dangers of being reluctantly drawn into a conflict with China or the Soviet Union over Taiwan. Indeed, the Truman administration's initial distancing from Taipei in the early years of the Cold War was partly intended to avoid this possibility. Likewise, Truman's successor Dwight Eisenhower was also wary, refusing repeated requests from Taipei to back a large-scale invasion to retake the mainland. Nonetheless, Washington did ultimately support Taipei in the crises of 1954–55 and 1958, threatening the use of nuclear weapons in the first instance and deploying US ships to break a Chinese blockade in the second.[46]

Taiwan's salience to a new US–China cold war could conceivably trigger conflict in at least one of three ways. Firstly, this flashpoint could come to be regarded as a 'litmus test' for Washington's willingness to support its allies and partners in the face of an increasingly powerful and assertive China. During the Taiwan Strait crisis of 1954–55, for instance, senior US officials – most notably then-secretary of state John Foster Dulles – were concerned that failure to defend Taiwan's offshore islands would deliver a devastating psychological blow to the fledgling US network of Asian alliances, raising questions over Washington's commitment.[47]

Although Taiwan is no longer a formal US ally, this argument continues to resonate. Tokyo, for instance, harbours concerns regarding US commitment should conflict break out between China and Japan – particularly over the disputed Senkaku/Diaoyu Islands in the East China Sea. In April 2014, Barack Obama thus became the first sitting US president to confirm publicly that the US–Japan Security Treaty extended to a contingency in this contested zone.[48] Then US secretary of defense James Mattis reiterated this pledge on a tour through Asia in February 2017.[49] Washington's unwillingness to come to Taiwan's defence could reinforce Tokyo's fears, however, especially if the lack of US support ultimately resulted in the island's involuntary reunification with the mainland. Some commentators even go so far as to suggest that such an outcome would cause Tokyo to terminate the US–Japan alliance.[50] Certainly when the Clinton administration deployed two aircraft-carrier battle groups at the height of the 1995–96 crisis, it was concerned that the United States' credibility as this region's 'security guarantor' might otherwise be called into question.[51]

Secondly, Taiwan's geostrategic significance to Sino-American competition might also convince US policymakers of the need to come to its defence. During the early years of the Cold War, for instance, Taiwan was regarded as a key link in a chain of islands – starting with the Aleutians and running down to the Philippines – which could be used to fence in the Communist bloc as part of a larger US containment strategy. The indomitable US general, Douglas MacArthur, went further still, famously characterising the island during the Korean War (1950–53) as an 'unsinkable aircraft carrier' that could serve as a base for operations aimed at retaking Asian territories under Communist rule as part of a 'rollback' strategy.[52] During the Cold War, US strategists also pointed to the dangers of allowing the island to fall into Soviet hands given its location close to sea lanes connecting America to Northeast Asia, and Japan to Southeast Asia.[53]

Similar considerations might motivate a decision to defend the island today. Some US commentators argue that keeping China boxed inside the so-called 'first island chain'

– which stretches from the Japanese home islands, through the Ryukyus and Taiwan, and down to the Philippines archipelago – is vital to winning the Sino-American strategic competition.[54] Others point to the strategic folly of allowing the island to fall into Beijing's hands, not only because this would surrender access to Taiwan's considerable economic resources, but also because it would allow China to project its military power much further into the Western Pacific by figuratively extending its coastline some 400 km eastward. As Denny Roy observes,

> Controlling Taiwan would provide the PRC with a massive platform for air and naval bases, an extension of the Chinese coastline ... and unfettered access to the Pacific Ocean from Taiwan's east coast. This would offer PLA forces a commanding position from which to control the western Pacific and to threaten U.S. bases on Okinawa or a U.S. Navy task force sailing in from the East.'[55]

Thirdly, the US might redeploy military assets closer to Taiwan as part of a new cost-imposition strategy towards China – this, too, would raise the risks of escalation. According to US analyst Thomas Mahnken, such strategies are designed to 'change a competitor's decision-making calculus and thus its strategic behaviour'. Typically imposed during peacetime, they 'can, and often do, involve the use of military assets but focus on the latent use of force to deter or coerce rather than to defeat competitors'.[56] During the Cold War, for instance, Eisenhower ended US patrols of the Taiwan Strait in February 1953, partly to complicate Chinese decision-making in the Korean War. Although these patrols were originally intended to deter Mao from invading Taiwan, they also prevented Chiang

Kai-shek from launching an attack in the opposite direction.[57] Eisenhower's withdrawal of the US Seventh Fleet from the Strait rekindled that possibility.

Chinese military modernisation from the mid-1990s also focused upon deterring Taiwanese independence and on developing the capability to deliver an effective military response should deterrence fail. A significant (and possibly unintended) consequence of the thaw in cross-strait relations from the late 2000s was that it allowed Beijing to deploy its military assets further afield – most notably into the East and South China seas. However, if Washington were to draw inspiration from Eisenhower's approach and now shifted more of its own military assets closer to the island – or even based them on the island itself, as has been suggested[58] – this could pressure Beijing into refocusing its energies back here as well, thereby challenging its continued capacity to deploy the same level of forces at greater distance. In the current atmosphere of deepening Sino-American strategic competition, and given the sensitivity of the Taiwan issue as a Chinese 'core interest', such a move would be highly provocative to Beijing.

History does not repeat itself, and it is important not to overdraw similarities between the Cold War and contemporary Sino-American competition. As international-relations scholar David Kang has demonstrated, great care needs to be taken when applying historical metaphors to Asia today.[59] Unlike the United States and the Soviet Union, who had minimal economic interaction, for instance, the Chinese and US economies are deeply interconnected – ongoing frictions over trade notwithstanding. Likewise, the leaderships of the two countries engage in regular dialogue aimed at reducing the prospects for strategic misperception, unlike during much of the Cold War. There are also extensive people-to-people links between the two societies: approximately 360,000 Chinese students, for example, are currently studying at universities in the US.[60] That said, the experience of the Cold War nonetheless highlights the potential for military escalation over Taiwan should it once again become a key battleground in the growing Sino-American contest for supremacy.

Military-technical incentives

Were a Sino-American clash to occur over Taiwan, the military-technical incentives for either side to escalate could be considerable. One choice that Washington would face very early on in such a crisis would be whether to target China's nuclear-armed submarines. This is a viable option for the US given that China's nuclear submarines remain acoustically noisy.[61] For Beijing to have a sea-based deterrent capability in a Taiwan contingency, however, it would need to have at least one of its small fleet of *Jin*-class nuclear-powered ballistic-missile submarines (SSBNs) beyond the first island chain and out in deeper waters, preferably within striking range of the continental United States.[62]

Should Washington opt not to engage China's nuclear submarines if and when it had the opportunity to do so, this would afford Beijing a second-strike capability. Yet were the US to target a Chinese nuclear submarine to prevent it, for instance, breaking out of the first island chain, this would constitute a significant escalation and one that would invite a commensurate Chinese response – particularly if Beijing perceived this as part of a more ambitious attempt to eliminate its nuclear capability altogether. Moreover, this could happen by accident rather than by design if the US were to mistake a Chinese nuclear submarine for an attack submarine. Although US capabilities have undoubtedly improved, target identification has historically proven to be one of the most demanding aspects of anti-submarine warfare (ASW). This contingency poses further difficulties, as the operating environment would likely be crowded.[63]

If the US attacked China's nuclear submarines, Beijing could quickly face the question of whether to cross the nuclear threshold or risk losing its second-strike capability. But there are other equally plausible avenues along which this point could be reached. Caitlin Talmadge has recently observed that the physical intermingling of China's conventional military forces and its relatively small nuclear arsenal – the DF21 missile, for instance, can carry either conventional or nuclear warheads and it is hard to accurately discern, especially at significant distance, which it is carrying – makes it difficult to target the former without threatening the latter. According to Talmadge,

> If U.S. operations endangered or damaged China's nuclear forces, Chinese leaders might come to think that Washington had aims beyond winning the conventional war – that it might be seeking to disable or destroy China's nuclear arsenal outright, perhaps as a prelude to regime change. In the fog of war, Beijing might reluctantly conclude that limited nuclear escalation – an initial strike small enough that it could avoid full-scale retaliation – was a viable option to defend itself.[64]

China's long-standing 'no first use' nuclear pledge might prevent such a scenario, although there is absolutely no guarantee that it would. Added to this, former US Pacific commander Admiral Dennis Blair claims that it is possible to distinguish Chinese nuclear submarines from their conventional counterparts and that US war planners are acutely aware of the dangers associated with targeting another state's nuclear arsenal.[65] Yet even Blair is forced to concede that Talmadge's scenario cannot be written off completely, because 'there is always a chance for an isolated mistake'.[66]

In a deepening crisis or conflict scenario, Beijing and Washington might also see advantages in pre-emptively targeting one another's satellites. US war-fighting capabilities are highly reliant upon space support systems, which in large part explains Beijing's efforts to augment its own military space programme in the aftermath of the 1995–96 Taiwan Strait crisis. While the details of this programme remain shrouded in secrecy, there is little doubt that it is progressing rapidly. Of particular relevance to a Taiwan contingency, Beijing is known to be producing a range of counter-space capabilities – including the anti-satellite missiles it first tested in January 2007, when it controversially destroyed a defunct weather satellite and, more recently, when it conducted a 'non-destructive' anti-satellite test in July 2014. China is also thought to be developing satellite jammers and directed-energy weapons that it could use to deny the US use of its space-based assets.[67]

The US could be equally tempted to eliminate Chinese satellites in order to blunt Beijing's ability to target its much-vaunted anti-shipping missiles beyond the first island chain. This possibility, in turn, could create compelling military-technical incentives for China to again embrace a 'use them or lose them' mentality. Such a chain of events seems unduly provocative and, indeed, almost inconceivable in peacetime conditions. Yet much can change in the heat of crisis. As Goldstein cautions,

> the effectiveness of the most advanced conventional weapons is tied to sophisticated command, control, communications, computers, intelligence, surveillance, and reconnaissance (C4ISR) networks that can be degraded through kinetic strikes or electronic and cyberwarfare … If, as is generally believed, emerg-

ing cyber- and space-warfare capabilities favor the attacker over the defender, once peacetime restraint based on mutual vulnerability gives way to the search for advantage in a crisis, neither side can be confident about the durability of its C4ISR.[68]

Goldstein's observation regarding the cyber domain is especially relevant to crisis stability over Taiwan. The US and China – and, indeed, Taiwan – have moved to improve both their offensive and defensive cyber-warfare capabilities. Yet they also continue to exhibit critical defensive vulnerabilities in this area which could, in turn, create powerful incentives for their opponent to move early and robustly in a conflict. China's A2/AD capabilities are increasingly reliant upon computer networks that the US would almost certainly attack in the event of major hostilities. Likewise, while US C4ISR systems are well protected, Beijing knows that slowing or potentially even preventing military US intervention in a Taiwan crisis could hinge upon their ability to disrupt these systems. This would require an overwhelming cyber attack which would also need to occur in the early stages of a crisis, particularly if Beijing was aiming to deter US involvement altogether. However, because cyber warfare is by nature ambiguous, it would be difficult (if not impossible) for the US to discern whether such an attack was an isolated act or a prelude to a major conventional strike. The US might thus respond to an overwhelming Chinese cyber attack with an immediate resort to armed conflict, believing major war to be imminent.[69]

Scholars Robert Ayson and Desmond Ball argued in 2014 that the increasingly interdependent C4ISR systems of the US and Japan – including the SOSUS arrays, which stretch from the Ryukyu Islands through to Taiwan and track Chinese submarines – could see Washington dragged into a Sino-Japanese conflict. In their words, if 'China fears that a major conflict with Japan is likely, it will have every reason to target these systems early on, in order to close the capability gap between the PLA and the [Japanese Self Defense Force]. But it will be very difficult for China to accomplish this without stimulating a response from the US.'[70]

A variation of this argument can be applied to the case at hand: Tokyo's involvement in a Taiwan contingency could well prove decisive. Japan would bring formidable air and naval forces to hostilities, as well as potent capabilities in the key area of anti-submarine warfare, where it remains second to none.[71] Japan's involvement is by no means a foregone conclusion. Tokyo has traditionally maintained an ambiguous position over Taiwan, often keeping a degree of distance during periods of crisis, calling for restraint from all parties and positioning itself as a potential intermediary.[72] In recent years, however, Tokyo's relations with both the United States and Taiwan have deepened, driven in large part by China's more aggressive behaviour.[73] Against that backdrop, it is increasingly difficult to imagine that Tokyo would not be drawn into a future Taiwan Strait crisis on the side of Washington and Taipei, especially so – applying Ayson and Ball's logic – if China were to attack US air bases on Okinawa or joint US–Japan C4ISR systems.

Dangers of complacency

No two epidemics have the same tipping point. That is why Gladwell was concerned primarily with the process by which a tipping point is reached, rather than the tipping point itself. Moreover, not every disease reaches epidemic proportions, just as not every idea, behaviour or product becomes a trend. The same is true for the Taiwan flashpoint. It is conceivable that it may remain dormant for some time yet and, indeed, that full-blown conflict might never break out. The prospect of nuclear escalation may instil caution; so might the prohibitive costs of conflict, or the uncertainty of its outcome. Cooler heads may yet prevail. None of this, however, should be cause for complacency. The potential pathways to this flashpoint's tipping point are multiple. If anything, they are becoming more likely. And there is little reason to anticipate a reversal of this increasingly dangerous trajectory.

CHAPTER FOUR

Policy options

North Korea has long been dubbed 'the land of lousy options', due to the paucity of workable policy options for dealing with this protracted problem.[1] A similar description increasingly applies to Taiwan. This chapter surveys and assesses the policy options most commonly contemplated in relation to this flashpoint: firstly, it outlines potential diplomatic approaches, including a cross-strait peace treaty, China's preferred 'one country, two systems' model, or a 'grand bargain' between China and the US. Secondly, it considers an enhanced US commitment to defend the island. Finally, it considers armed conflict. None of these options are attractive. In the absence of any definitive, near-term solution to this flashpoint, it points to the pressing need for new crisis-management mechanisms for navigating the dangerous decade ahead.

Diplomatic avenues

With diplomacy making unexpected headway on the Korean Peninsula during 2018–19, it is worth considering whether the Taiwan flashpoint could follow a similar path. This observation may initially seem out of place in a book arguing that the risks of armed conflict over Taiwan are intensifying. But it is worth making the point that during 2017, the Korean Peninsula also drifted dangerously close to war – as epitomised by US President Donald Trump's threats in August of that year to unleash upon Pyongyang 'fire and fury like the world has never seen'.[2] This came before North Korea's 'charm offensive' at the 2018 Winter Olympics in Pyeongchang, which led to an unanticipated thawing in inter-Korean relations and two summits between Trump and North Korean leader Kim Jong-un. Moreover, as peace processes past in Aceh, Cambodia and Northern Ireland suggest, conflict resolution can sometimes spring from the most unlikely of circumstances.

Peace agreement

Of the diplomatic possibilities previously canvassed for the Taiwan flashpoint, the idea of a cross-strait peace agreement was first proposed as early as 2005, when then-opposition leader of the Kuomintang (KMT) Lien Chan made a historic visit to the mainland to meet with then Chinese president Hu Jintao, in his capacity as leader of the Chinese Communist Party (CCP). Hu reiterated the possibility of a peace agreement in his October 2007 address to China's National Party Congress, as did KMT candidate Ma Ying-jeou and his Democratic Progressive Party (DPP) opponent Frank Hsieh while campaigning in the run-up to Taiwan's January 2008 presidential election. When the KMT then reclaimed the presidency, Ma clarified that a peace agreement would not be on the cards during his first term in office, but that he would seek to negotiate one should he win a second term.[3] Although Ma subsequently made the same pledge in advance of the island's January 2012 presidential election, he reneged on this promise and the KMT removed the idea from its party platform altogether in August 2017, as it sought to win back voters following its landslide electoral defeat.[4]

Nonetheless, the idea of a peace agreement persists. Most recently, KMT chairman Wu Den-yih unexpectedly indicated during a February 2019 interview that if his party regained the presidency in 2020, it would seek to negotiate a peace treaty with the mainland.[5] What exactly any such peace agreement would consist of remains unclear. It could conceivably be a relatively informal arrangement entailing oral understandings reached through negotiations but not committed to writing; and the specifics of the agreement could remain private rather than being publicly articulated. Such an arrangement might be easier to negotiate, but it could also be much harder to enforce than the alternative of a formal, written peace treaty.[6]

The scope of any putative China–Taiwan peace agreement is the subject of much debate. In the past, some have suggested a minimalist approach, envisaging a Taiwanese pledge not to formally declare independence in return for a commitment from Beijing not to use military force against the island. As with the ongoing inter-Korean peace process, a step up from this option could involve a small number of concrete steps from Beijing to demonstrate commitment to such a deal – for example, the withdrawal of some of its missiles from Fujian province opposite Taiwan. A more ambitious agreement might involve the inclusion of economic incentives akin to those pursued during Ma's presidency – such as increased trade or transport links – along with measures to improve the flow of people, information and ideas across the strait.[7]

However, before issues of nature and scope can even begin to be addressed, at least three significant challenges will need to be surmounted. The prospects for doing so at present are not promising. Firstly, Xi Jinping and Tsai Ing-wen are distinctly unlikely to engage in the kind of high-level summitry witnessed between Trump and Kim. That said, the DPP has not completely ruled out a cross-strait peace agreement. In

November 2016, for instance, a Tsai government spokesperson indicated that the administration would be open to such an arrangement, provided international backing and domestic support on Taiwan was in place, and that China did not stipulate any political preconditions for peace talks.[8] This latter requirement is a sticking point for Beijing, however, which remains adamant that cross-strait negotiations hinge upon the willingness of Taipei to accept the 1992 Consensus as Beijing understands it. Tsai has repeatedly ruled out that possibility, arguing that Taiwan never accepted Beijing's interpretation of the 'one China' policy. Indeed, for Tsai to give ground on this position now would be political suicide, especially since Taiwan's status as a 'sovereign and independent country' has been part of the DPP's party platform since 1999.[9]

Given that proposals for a peace agreement have traditionally been associated with the KMT, Beijing might still seek negotiations via this route, in anticipation of their regaining the presidency as early as 2020. This is consistent with the approach taken when the idea of a peace agreement was first formally proposed. However, the DPP is alert to this possibility and has actively sought to shut it down. When then-leader of the KMT Hung Hsiu-chu visited the mainland in late 2016 to meet with Xi, for instance, Tsai's Mainland Affairs Council minister Katharine Chang stated publicly that the visit was not official and that Hung had no authority to conclude any agreement with Beijing, whether a peace treaty or signing up to the 1992 Consensus.[10]

Secondly, it is not clear that sufficient domestic political support exists for a peace agreement on either side of the Taiwan Strait, or that leaders in Beijing or Taipei would be willing to take the risks needed to generate it. While domestic factors were important in the KMT's resounding 2016 electoral defeat, Ma's rapprochement with Beijing undoubtedly proved damaging. Domestic anger at Ma's diplomacy gained its clearest expression in the Sunflower Movement of 2014.

Reflecting this widespread lack of support for a peace agreement, DPP legislators in February 2019 proposed a new amendment to the act governing relations between Taiwan and the mainland. This amendment requires that a national referendum be held before any China–Taiwan peace agreement can be formally signed.[11] Xi, by behaving as a strongman at home and abroad, has limited his options for any peace agreement with Taiwan's current leadership. Having already established clear preconditions for negotiations with Tsai, any flexibility from Xi could be read within China as a sign of weakness, thus undermining Xi's reputation as leader and potentially even posing a threat to his political survival.

Thirdly, even in the unlikely event that a peace agreement was reached, Beijing and Taipei would each harbour legitimate concerns regarding its sustainability. For Taipei, its biggest worry is that the mainland could renege on the deal if the cross-strait and US–China military balances have moved decisively in its favour. Equally, the very realisation that these power relativities are continuing to shift may further dampen Beijing's appetite for negotiations to begin with. As US analysts Philip Saunders and Scott Kastner presciently argued a decade ago:

> One potential obstacle involves the future balance of power: to the extent that long-term trends mostly favour China, a peace agreement might simply postpone Taiwan's day of reckoning while foreclosing the island's options … Given that China will likely be stronger in the future, Chinese leaders have limited incentives to make concessions if they believe they will win in the long run.[12]

Beijing, too, would have understandable concerns over Taiwan's reliability as a negotiating partner. Even if China were to strike a peace agreement with a future KMT-led government, there would be no guarantee that the DPP would not revoke this deal if it returned to power.

One country, two systems

The 'one country, two systems' model has gained renewed prominence following Xi's address in January 2019 – his first dedicated specifically to Taiwan – in which he called for the island's reunification with the mainland according to this formula.[13] As detailed in Chapter One, when Deng Xiaoping originally proposed the one country, two systems model in 1981, Taiwan was foremost in his mind. But the one country, two systems proposal met a cool reception on the island. The CCP was widely viewed as a 'bandit regime', with Deng's proposal seen as a deceptive ploy for 'peaceful annexation'.[14] Quickly recognising the extent of resistance and the short-term futility of applying his formula to the island, Deng turned his attention to Hong Kong and, by late 1981, had fleshed out a proposal for its employment there. One country, two systems became a central element of the December 1984 Sino-British Joint Declaration, which outlined arrangements for Hong Kong's reversion to China in July 1997.[15]

Two subsequent developments further hardened Taiwanese resistance to the one country, two systems formula. The first was the island's democratisation. Under Hong Kong's Constitution – known as the 'Basic Law' – Beijing retained significant influence over the selection of Hong Kong's chief executive and its Legislative Council. As the US analyst Richard Bush observes,

> In crafting the provisions of the Hong Kong Basic Law on how the chief executive and members of the

Legislative Council were to be selected, Beijing had made sure that it retained significant control over who was picked and who, thereafter, dominated the legislative process.[16]

One country, two systems has been applied differently in Hong Kong than in Macau, where it was introduced relatively easily following the reversion of the former Portuguese colony to the mainland in December 1999. However, scepticism understandably abounds on Taiwan as to whether Beijing would ultimately permit a leader like Tsai or a party like the DPP to hold office under one country, two systems.

Secondly, Hong Kong's experience has reinforced Taiwanese scepticism of reunification. As recently as 2013, the possibility of electoral reform allowing for popular elections was still being entertained in Hong Kong. However, those hopes were ultimately never realised. In response, the Umbrella Movement – which saw tens of thousands of pro-democracy demonstrators take to Hong Kong's streets for 79 days, drawing some inspiration from Taiwan's Sunflower Movement – erupted in September 2014. Beijing's curtailment of political and civil freedoms in Hong Kong has only tightened during the period since. Chinese agents have famously seized Hong Kong booksellers critical of the CCP, while Hong Kong's government has arrested pro-democracy activists, blocked opposition politicians from office and even banned a political party for its advocacy of Hong Kong's independence.[17] An increasingly tense situation finally combusted in June 2019, when protests that began in February and March in response to proposed legislation allowing Hong Kong's government to extradite criminal suspects to the mainland, Macau and Taiwan escalated significantly.[18] As such, while Deng had hoped that the successful implementation of the one country, two systems model to Hong Kong would eventually entice Taiwan down the same path, its application has instead created a strong impression that 'one country' has taken clear precedence over the 'two systems'.

Consistent with this, public-opinion polling conducted in January 2019 found that 80.9% of Taiwanese rejected the one country, two systems model as a basis for cross-strait relations. This view was even evident among self-identifying KMT voters, 64.7% of whom opposed the formula.[19] Interestingly, another poll of Hong Kong residents conducted the same month found a similar level of scepticism regarding the model's applicability to Taiwan. In this instance, 59% of those surveyed believed that one country, two systems would not work in Taiwan, while only 29% thought that it could.[20] Accordingly, Tsai's unequivocal rebuke of Xi's address was unsurprising: 'It is impossible for me or, in my view, any responsible politician in Taiwan to accept President Xi Jinping's recent remarks without betraying the trust and the will of the people of Taiwan.'[21] Likewise, the KMT's normally pro-China presidential candidate, Han Kuo-yu, has indicated publicly that one country, two systems would only come into effect 'over his dead body'.[22]

Grand bargain

Tsai's government has pushed back strongly against Taiwan becoming a bargaining chip in a Sino-American grand bargain. Taipei's fears regarding this possibility have become more acute since Trump's election, given his reputation as a self-styled 'deal maker'. Trump himself inadvertently fuelled these anxieties during an interview with the *Wall Street Journal* published in January 2017, during which he indicated that 'everything is under negotiation including One China', contingent upon reform in Beijing's trade and currency practices.[23] Although some commentators saw this as favourable to Taiwan, it is possible to read it another way. This became more apparent when Trump agreed the next month to honour the One China policy during a phone conversation with Xi; moreover, as tensions heightened on the Korean Peninsula throughout 2017, speculation mounted that Trump might trade Beijing's support for reining in Pyongyang in return for the US distancing itself from Taiwan.[24] More recent revelations from a January 2018 National Security Council meeting, in which Trump reportedly asked 'what do we get from protecting Taiwan?', have only heightened Taipei's anxieties.[25]

The idea of a Sino-American grand bargain in which the US abandons Taiwan is not new. Indeed, this was arguably the exact path taken by Nixon and Kissinger when the US normalised diplomatic relations with China during the 1970s.[26] More recently, the US scholar Charles Glaser has argued that Washington should re-evaluate and, ultimately, end its commitment to defending Taiwan, in return for a pledge from Beijing to resolve its disputes in the East and the South China seas peacefully, and to accept formally the United States' security role in Asia – including its alliances and forward-deployed military forces.[27] Lyle Goldstein has sketched out an even more elaborate scheme in which Washington might make a series of concessions on Taiwan – including revealing to Beijing the full extent of its military ties with the island, closing the office of its military representative in the American Institute in Taiwan (AIT), curtailing US arms sales and pushing for a resolution to the dispute. In return, Beijing would take a series of reciprocal steps, including engaging in cross-strait confidence-building measures without preconditions, removing short-range and cruise missiles currently within 1,000 kilometres of the island, restricting construction of its amphibious fleet and renouncing the use of force.[28]

As distasteful as many of Taiwan's supporters find it, the idea of substantially reducing Washington's security commitment to the island cannot be dismissed entirely, especially if enforceable Chinese concessions could be extracted in return. It would serve to circumvent one of the thorniest, most combustible issues in the increasingly tense relationship between China and the US. But, more importantly, if executed gradually, a reduction in America's defence commitment to Taiwan would also wean Taipei off US support before Washington is no longer able to credibly offer that assistance. That day might well be approaching far sooner than Taipei and Washington may wish to acknowledge.

But even if there is a case that the US *should* reduce its long-standing security commitment to Taiwan, it remains unlikely that it would do so willingly. First and foremost, domestic political obstacles stand in the way. As the enactment of the Taiwan Relations Act (TRA) highlights, Taipei has traditionally enjoyed strong support in the US Congress. While that support eased somewhat during the mid-1990s, as Taiwan's legendary lobbying efforts on Capitol Hill declined, it has since recovered and may now be stronger than ever – as evinced by the 2018 Taiwan Travel Act and the 2019 National Defense Authorization Act (NDAA). If the US were to step back significantly from its existing security commitments to Taiwan, this would almost certainly require amendment – and possibly even the rescinding – of the TRA. The congressional support required for such a step would not be forthcoming. Indeed, in May 2019 the House of Representatives unanimously passed the Taiwan Assurance Act, which describes the island as 'a vital part of the United States [*sic*] free and open Indo-Pacific strategy' and which reaffirms US commitment to implementing the TRA.[29]

An interrelated set of moral considerations also reduce the prospects for US abandonment. When Nixon and Kissinger effectively betrayed Taiwan during the 1970s, the island was still under the authoritarian rule of Chiang's KMT. Abandoning a democratic Taiwan today, however, is an entirely different proposition. Moreover, it is one that would be seen to violate long-standing and deeply held American principles. As US scholar Aaron Friedberg articulates,

> Whatever considerations led to America's initial separation from the island in the 1970's, to consign it now to the tender mercies of the mainland would be a disgrace. Taiwan has, after all, remade itself into precisely the kind of society that Americans say they favor and wish to promote around the world. To abandon a fellow democracy in hopes of commercial and geopolitical gain, or even out of a well-intentioned wish to preserve the peace, would starkly violate American principles.[30]

Opponents of reducing US commitment to Taiwan also cite a host of strategic reasons. They suggest, for example, that such a course would only embolden Beijing and undermine the entire US alliance network in Asia as Tokyo, Seoul and even Canberra would all have reason to doubt America's reliability and resolve. This is a somewhat dubious claim, of course, given that the formal treaty arrangements that the US has with these three countries technically carry greater weight than its much looser commitments to Taiwan. However, critics of abandonment also point to Taiwan's central location in the strategically significant island chain stretching from Japan down to the South China Sea. Ceding this advantageous position to the mainland, they contend, would provide Beijing with its own unsinkable aircraft carrier, thus further enhancing its ability to project military power across the entire Western Pacific.[31]

Were the US to further loosen its ties with Taiwan, this could also induce the island to undertake radical strategic responses.

The prospect of Taiwan developing a nuclear-weapons capability would be a particularly severe outcome. There is clear historical precedent: in response to China's first nuclear-weapons test, in October 1964, Taipei commenced its own nuclear-weapons programme under the cover of the newly established Institute for Nuclear Energy Research (INER). The programme was quickly put under US surveillance, while inspections conducted by the International Atomic Energy Agency (IAEA) in 1976–77 revealed discrepancies between Taiwan's declared and actual nuclear activities. Washington protested and Taipei pledged to shut the programme down – which it eventually appears to have done in the late 1970s. The programme, however, restarted in the mid-1980s. By this time, Taiwan was reportedly only one to two years away from acquiring a nuclear-weapons capability when Col Chang Hsien-yi – deputy director of the INER and a long-standing Central Intelligence Agency (CIA) asset – left Taiwan for the US and exposed its existence.[32] Preventing the reconstitution of Taiwan's nuclear programme today is a rare point of agreement between Beijing and Washington. Both sides would likely take steps to stop such a development – potentially, in China's case, involving the use of military force.

Enhanced deterrence

As detailed in Chapter Two, Taiwan's efforts to develop asymmetric military capabilities – mines, missiles and smaller, stealthier platforms – have intensified over the past decade. Their aim is to deter a Chinese amphibious assault by substantially raising the costs and risks to the mainland. Many of Taiwan's supporters, however, argue that the island cannot deter an increasingly powerful China alone. The best chance for resisting Chinese coercion and deterring conflict, they argue, lies in America deepening ties and enhancing its commitment to Taiwan.

In its most extreme form, the enhanced-deterrence argument suggests that Washington should abandon strategic ambiguity altogether, replacing it with an ironclad, alliance-like security guarantee to Taiwan. Its advocates also often argue that the US should visibly strengthen its capabilities for deterring China and defending the island. This could potentially involve deploying additional military forces in the Indo-Pacific, as well as encouraging allies and partners to engage in military exercises with these forces. Some commentators suggest that the US could further demonstrate its commitment to Taiwan by substantially improving defensive measures at US military bases currently vulnerable to Chinese missile attack. One proposal, for instance, argues for increasing the number of hardened aircraft shelters at Kadena Air Base on Okinawa.[33]

Enhanced deterrence might also entail a more visible US military presence on and around Taiwan itself. The 2018 NDAA, for instance, indicated that the US should 'consider the advisability and feasibility of re-establishing port of call exchanges between the United States Navy and the Taiwan Navy'.[34] A Washington-based Chinese diplomat, Li Kexin, famously responded to this development by asserting that 'the day that a U.S. Navy vessel arrives in Kaohsiung is the day that our People's Liberation Army unifies Taiwan with military force'.[35] But advocates of an enhanced-deterrence strategy argue that Washington should not be dissuaded by such threats. Instead, they believe that the US needs to continue developing more advanced weapons platforms and new operational concepts designed to demonstrate its ability to come to Taiwan's defence if necessary.[36] Such proposals generally stop short of proposing an actual US military presence on Taiwan, on grounds that this would be unduly provocative to Beijing.

Advocates of an enhanced-deterrence strategy also argue that the US needs to further support Taiwan's ability to defend itself. These arguments often emphasise US arms sales to the island, which enhanced-deterrence advocates argue need to become more normalised and regularised.[37] In a similar vein, they maintain that the US should allow Taiwan access to more advanced military platforms, including submarines and the F-35 Joint Strike Fighter.[38] They also call upon the US to assist Taiwan with developing innovative new defence strategies, and for the inclusion of Taiwan's armed forces in military exercises – both bilateral and multilateral – with their US counterparts. Even before China was dis-invited to the US-led *Rim of the Pacific* (RIMPAC) naval exercises in May 2018, for instance, supporters of closer US–Taiwan defence ties had called for Taiwan's inclusion.[39] An earlier draft of the NDAA went further still, proposing US participation in Taiwan's annual *Han Kuang* exercises, although this clause was ultimately removed from an otherwise decidedly pro-Taiwan piece of legislation.[40]

Enhanced-deterrence advocates also call for greater US support for Taiwan beyond the narrow military domain. The suggestion has been made, for example, to improve Taiwan's deterrence capabilities through increasing its resilience to Chinese cyber intrusions and political-influence campaigns.[41] US analysts Dan Blumenthal and Michael Mazza have proposed the prioritising of a US–Taiwan free-trade agreement (FTA), with a view to reducing Taiwan's economic dependence on the mainland. In their words,

> Closer U.S.–Taiwan ties across the board, including in the economic relationship, would contribute to ... dissuading Beijing from further unsettling actions, and ensuring that this crucial neck of the Indo-Pacific woods remains free. The U.S. has a vital interest in

cross-strait stability, and that can only be assured if the people of Taiwan believe they will not be overwhelmed economically by Beijing.[42]

In a variation on this theme, RAND analyst Michael Chase suggests that the US should actively assist Taipei in diversifying its economic relationships, including through helping Taiwan to join the Comprehensive and Progressive Agreement for Trans-Pacific Partnership (CPTPP). The CPTPP is a revised version of the Trans-Pacific Partnership (TPP), which Trump infamously withdrew from in January 2017 during his first day in office.[43]

As with diplomatic approaches, however, these options for enhanced deterrence have considerable downsides. For deterrence to succeed, Beijing ultimately needs to be convinced that America is *willing* to risk major conflict – potentially including a nuclear exchange – to defend Taiwan.[44] It is far from clear that this is currently the case. Indeed, despite the pro-Taiwan orientation of some in his administration – such as National Security Advisor John Bolton and Assistant Secretary of Defense Randall Schriver – Trump's 'America First' posture sends precisely the opposite message. His announcement in December 2018 of a complete and immediate withdrawal of US forces from Syria – partially reversed the following March – coupled with Trump's threats to draw down US troops from the Korean Peninsula and questioning of the alliance with Japan, have led Beijing to wonder how far Washington would go to defend Taiwan.[45] And it is important to bear in mind that such uncertainties existed prior to Trump: Washington's unwillingness to intervene following Moscow's incursions into Georgia in 2008 and its annexation of Crimea in 2014 sowed the initial seeds of doubt. As in these cases, Beijing today could quite understandably draw the conclusion that the US may not be willing to incur the rapidly rising costs and risks of major-power war to defend Taiwan.

The success of enhanced deterrence also rests upon China being convinced that the US is *able* to come to Taiwan's defence. While the US probably retains that ability at present, as discussed, its capacity to defend Taiwan appears set to erode over the course of the next decade as China's overall military weight, and its anti-access and area-denial (A2/AD) capabilities in particular, further improve. It is possible – as advocates of enhanced deterrence suggest – that America will successfully counter these trends by developing new, advanced weapons systems and operational concepts. However, such hopes need to be set against the backdrop of a US federal budget that is under severe stress. Almost 70% of that budget is already committed to so-called 'mandatory' expenditures, including funding for Social Security, Medicare and Medicaid. The Pentagon already receives approximately half of the remaining 30% available for so-called 'discretionary' spending. As such, despite calls for further defence-budget increases from some quarters, these are likely to be modest at best in the years to come. Indeed, the Pentagon has reportedly been told to brace for a 'flattening out' of defence expenditure.[46]

Even if the US could find additional defence funding for enhanced-deterrence options, Beijing could, and probably would, move quickly to counter improvements in US military capabilities. Short of a transformational, and presently unforeseen, technological breakthrough that it might struggle to match, China would have strong incentives to devote additional resources to its own defence budget to address US gains. Moreover, due to the advantages that the strategic geography of this flashpoint afford it, China would be able to do so at significantly lower cost than the US. Hence, as Eric Gomez of the Cato Institute has observed, if Beijing quickly offsets the advantages of a stronger U.S. military support for Taiwan, the United States could end up in a similar position to the one it's in now, but with a stronger China to deter.[47]

The US adoption of an enhanced-deterrence posture vis-à-vis Taiwan could also cause Sino-American relations to rapidly descend into what US scholar Robert Ross has described as 'exacerbated security dilemma dynamics'.[48] Would Washington – already standing at the precipice of what some commentators characterise as a new cold war with China – be willing and able to go down that path? The quiet demise in January 2015 of the controversial 'AirSea Battle' – an operational concept introduced in 2010 essentially to counter China's A2/AD capabilities – suggests not. One of the fundamental flaws of this concept was the assumption that China's key command-and-control targets could be eliminated without provoking rapid escalation to the nuclear level.[49]

More importantly, however, despite the hardening in attitudes towards China that has apparently occurred in Washington, the US still needs some level of cooperation from Beijing to address broader differences in their relationship over a range of issues including trade, cyber security, allegations of political influence and interference, and the South China Sea. Moreover, as China remains the source of as much as 90% of North Korea's international trade, Beijing's assistance or otherwise will also continue profoundly to affect Washington's ongoing efforts to address the North Korean nuclear challenge.[50] While resolutions of any of these issues seem improbable at this juncture, should the US introduce further animosity into relations with Beijing by significantly enhancing its ability to deter military action against Taiwan, China could in turn make life decidedly more difficult for Washington on a number of other fronts. Washington is unlikely to risk that outcome.

Catastrophic conflict

If diplomatic avenues and enhanced deterrence are ultimately not viable, could the Taiwan flashpoint instead be resolved by military force? As with the previous policy options, assessing the utility of military alternatives is complicated by the fact that force could be applied in a variety of ways. Beijing has the option of launching missiles and airstrikes against the island, of strangling it through a blockade, or of mounting a full-scale amphibious invasion. It could well use all three of these approaches together. But once military means are employed, the path hostilities could take would be subject to a wide range of variables, further complicating the assessment of military options. Would hostilities be limited to China and Taiwan, for instance, or would other players – such as the US and Japan – become involved? How long would the fighting last and how intense would it become? What would be the economic conse-quences, both for the parties engaged in direct hostilities and globally? How would domestic politics in each of these engaged polities play out? The answers to each of these questions have a critical bearing upon any assessment of military options.

China targets Taiwan with around 1,200 short-range ballis-tic missiles, 400 land-attack cruise missiles and an unknown number of medium-range ballistic missiles.[51] As detailed in Chapter Two, it also possesses a growing fleet of advanced fighter aircraft which it could use to attack the island. Such assets might serve a variety of purposes. Beijing could order missile strikes, for instance, to intimidate the population on Taiwan, with a view to coercing them into reunification. If the purpose of missile strikes was solely to influence public opinion in this way, it is likely that these would be intermittent, of relatively lower intensity and that they would be punctuated by periods of strategic pause to allow for the possibility of political negotiations.[52] Conversely, Chinese missile strikes could instead serve as a prelude to a full-scale invasion, in which case they would be of considerably higher intensity and aimed at carefully selected targets, including surface-to-air missile (SAM) batteries and early-warning radars, air and naval bases, and Taiwanese command posts. Such strikes would primarily aim to sufficiently degrade the island's air defence and other offensive capabilities to allow China to establish air superiority and sea control around Taiwan.[53]

Due to the vulnerability of Chinese ships and submarines to Taiwanese fighters, maritime-patrol aircraft and anti-submarine warfare (ASW) helicopters, achieving air superiority and sea control would be critical to Beijing's chances of successfully executing its second military option of a blockade. That said, the blockade option is still likely to hold considerable appeal for Beijing, given Taiwan's high level of dependence upon external food and fuel supplies. The island imports an estimated 80–90% of its food and its stockpile of key agricultural products would reportedly last for just four months. Likewise, Taiwan imports almost all of its oil and has only a 90-day stockpile of this critical resource.[54]

A Chinese blockade would probably focus upon Taiwan's seven major ports – four of which are positioned on the island's west coast, directly opposite the mainland.[55] Submarines and bombers would lay several belts of sea mines – at various depths and distances as far out as 10 nautical miles – to prevent ships coming to and leaving port. Ships that sought to leave or to return could be sunk, with a view to deterring others from running the blockade while, in a more extreme version of this scenario, ships in port and port infrastructure itself could also be destroyed. In addition to the focus upon sea mines, publicly available Chinese military writings have also discussed the possibility of a more elaborate multi-ringed blockade, where dense mine belts are supplemented with a ring of surface ships circling the island further out, and an additional ring of maritime-patrol aircraft enforcing the blockade from as far as 50 nautical miles away.[56]

Taiwanese are also heavily dependent on technology. In addition to strangling the island's food and fuel supplies, therefore, Beijing might seek to create widespread panic and confusion by shutting down its internet and communications networks. As discussed in Chapter Three, cyber warfare would almost certainly be a central element of China's third and most ambitious military option – a full-scale amphibious invasion of the island. Such an operation would be extremely difficult and dangerous to execute. Added to the aforementioned natural challenges that the island and its surrounds present to an invading force – steep cliffs, vast mud flats, demanding seas and highly inclement weather – Chinese forces would also need to neutralise Taiwan's offshore islands – the Kinmen and Matsu groups, the tiny fortress of Wu-qiu and the Penghu Islands (or Pescadores) – prior to commencing an invasion of the island proper. Failure to neutralise these features would leave the invading force vulnerable to attack as it continued its treacherous journey across the Taiwan Strait. It would also leave the mainland – especially the strategically significant port city of Fuzhou in Fujian province – open to Taiwanese missile strikes, helicopter assaults and even commando raids. Beijing would initially rely upon its own missile and artillery strikes to neutralise Taiwan's offshore islands. However, an 'on-the ground' military presence would ultimately be required to ensure that these strikes had been successful.[57]

While China's power-projection capabilities have improved markedly over the past two decades, it still lacks sufficient

military transport ships and aircraft to ferry sufficient personnel (perhaps as many as one million troops) across the strait.
As such, Beijing would need to rely upon a makeshift flotilla
of commercial ships and aircraft to execute what one analyst
has described as 'the largest amphibious operation in human
history'.[58] This would be highly risky on many levels. For one,
many if not most of the captains and pilots called upon will
have had no experience in high-intensity warfare. Their vessels
would move much more slowly than specialist military craft,
making them more vulnerable to attack. Communications
would also be fraught due to the challenge of information
management and overload across such a vast armada.

Assuming Chinese forces even made it to shore in sufficient
numbers, success of the amphibious invasion would still be
far from assured. Adding to the island's natural geographic
advantages, over the decades Taiwan has reportedly developed
an elaborate defensive system to thwart an attack from the sea.
This includes the capacity to deploy rapidly thick layers of sea
mines – so-called 'belts of death' – to protect the approaches
to the 13 beaches on Taiwan's west coast that are suitable for
landing.[59] Thick forests of steel pikes would be deployed along
these beaches to further impede the invading force. Most daunt-
ing of all, perhaps, Taiwan has also installed so-called 'seawalls
of fire' at these beaches – an elaborate system of underwater
pipelines that would spew oil and gas onto the advancing
forces, which would subsequently ignite in the heavy gunfire.[60]

Having made it ashore and secured at least one major
landing area, Chinese forces would then face the challenge of
moving inland to capture the island's major cities, especially
Taipei. Fighting would likely be intense and bloody. Faced
with the prospect of its extinction as a society, the possibility
has been mooted that Taiwan might resort to the use of crude
weapons of mass destruction – 'dirty' bombs, poisoned gas

and other biological agents – in a last-ditch attempt to stave off the invasion.[61] An alternative possibility is that the remnants of Taiwan's armed forces could retreat to the mountainous terrain in the centre of the island and on its rugged east coast, from where they would wage a guerrilla-style campaign.

It is possible, of course, that Taiwanese resistance would have faded long before this point. Questions have been raised regarding the resilience of Taiwanese born since 1978 – the so-called 'Strawberry Generation', who are stereotyped as 'beautiful but highly fragile and easily bruised'.[62] Yet history also suggests that only the most intense of military operations stands a chance of bringing about such capitulation. Political scientist Michael Beckley observes that 'no blockade in the past 200 years has coerced a country into surrendering its sovereignty. The reason is that modern states can adapt to supply shortages, and civilian populations are usually willing to endure enormous punishment to defy a foreign enemy.'[63] The same is true of strategic bombing campaigns. According to Beckley, of the 14 which have been conducted over the past two centuries, none of these *alone* has led to one country conquering another. Rather, bombing campaigns have traditionally succeeded only in hastening the demise of a polity already heading toward defeat, and have otherwise tended only to harden the resolve of the targeted population.[64]

The use of overwhelming military force against Taiwan, however, would also increase the prospects for third-party intervention. Were Beijing to execute a sustained blockade of the island that led to Taiwanese dying in large numbers, for instance, it would be hard to imagine that China would not attract widespread opprobrium, multilateral sanctions and perhaps even the assembly of a multinational coalition to break the blockade. Similarly, domestic political pressures – particularly from Taiwan's supporters in the US Congress – for the

US to respond militarily to a large-scale Chinese missile strike or amphibious invasion would likely be considerable. Beijing could seek to stymie the prospect of American intervention by conducting additional missile strikes against US assets deployed off the coast of China, as well as US military bases in Japan and Guam. However, such a step would run a high risk of provoking a muscular US military response, as well as potentially drawing Japan into the fray.

The costs of major-power conflict over Taiwan would also be prohibitive. A RAND study published in 2016, simulating a 'severe' US–China conflict in 2025 that could last for up to a year, suggested that both sides would suffer 'very heavy' military losses and neither would be able to establish decisive military–operational advantage.[65] If such a conflict erupted today, the economic costs would be equally devastating for both sides and, indeed, for the world. Almost all of China's trade would be disrupted, leading to an estimated 25–35% decline in its GDP. Given the growing number of Asian economies – including Australia, Indonesia, Japan, the Philippines and South Korea – that now count the Chinese market as their leading export destination, the knock-on effect of China's precipitous GDP decline would thus be considerable. Similarly, the costs to the US economy resulting from major Chinese cyber attacks during the conflict could be anywhere from US$70bn–US$900bn.[66] RAND also notes that even mild hostilities over the same 12-month period could generate 'serious economic harm', while the potential economic costs of severe conflict will most likely increase over the course of the next decade.[67]

The need for crisis management

A decade ago, hopes were high that so-called 'confidence-building measures' (CBMs) could be introduced to ameliorate the prospects of catastrophic cross-strait conflict, buoyed by the

KMT's return to power with Ma's election. The CBM concept itself is an amorphous one which can be used to describe a whole host of measures. Broad definitions encompass virtually any attempt to reduce tension, suspicion or uncertainty between or among disputants. CBMs can also focus more narrowly on the military domain. Here their intention is to increase transparency and predictability between opposing forces – through, for example, the exchange of information about doctrine, invitations to observe military exercises or the establishment of 'hotlines' between defence establishments – with a view to reducing the chances for misperception and/ or inadvertent escalation. CBMs are generally informal and non-binding, although they can be formal and binding – such as those developed by the Organization for Security and Co-operation in Europe (OSCE). They can be executed unilaterally, bilaterally or multilaterally.[68]

Cross-strait CBMs have a relatively long history, even if they have not always been defined in precisely those terms. As far back as 1990, for instance, the Red Cross societies of Taiwan and the mainland signed the so-called 'Kinmen Agreement', in which they pledged to cooperate in fighting crime across the Taiwan Strait and with the repatriation of illegal immigrants. Retired military officers from Taiwan and the mainland have also engaged in dialogue aimed at enhancing mutual understanding of security perceptions. Furthermore, in November 1997, Taiwan's China Rescue Association and the mainland's China Marine Rescue Center agreed to establish a civilian hotline which operated 24 hours a day and that could be used to help rescue ships in distress in the Taiwan Strait.[69] This development provided a precedent of sorts for the hotline agreed to by Xi and Ma in September 2015. In addition to these and other CBMs, Taiwan has also introduced CBMs unilaterally, such as announcing its major military exercises in advance.[70]

A long list of additional CBMs have previously been proposed, including by prominent US analysts such as Ralph Cossa and Brad Glosserman of Pacific Forum and Bonnie Glaser of the Center for Strategic and International Studies in Washington DC. The idea of a 'buffer zone' in the middle of the Taiwan Strait – which military ships and aircraft from both sides would avoid – has been floated.[71] Another suggestion is that the mainland publish details regarding the date, size, location and purpose of its military exercises, along similar lines to what Taiwan currently does.[72] A significantly more ambitious 'code of conduct' for preventing dangerous military activities – analogous to the 1972 Incidents at Sea agreement and the 1989 Dangerous Military Incidents accord between the US and the Soviet Union – has also been mooted for the Taiwan Strait, as have CBMs which extend into the areas of environmental protection and public health.[73]

Prospects for new cross-strait CBMs are currently poor. Indeed, given the typically informal and non-binding nature of such measures, just upholding those which have previously been agreed is challenging enough, as highlighted by China's March 2019 crossing of the hitherto tacitly acknowledged median line. Beijing's opposition to new CBMs is particularly acute, as it wants to avoid conferring legitimacy to Taiwan's DPP-led government, especially with Tsai ruling out any endorsement of the 1992 Consensus. Threats of military coercion also remain central to Beijing's strategy for deterring pro-independence sentiment on the island. Proposals such as those calling for a buffer zone in the middle of the Taiwan Strait are therefore unlikely to gain much traction while Beijing continues to rely upon displays of military power ever closer to the island as a coercive tactic.

Having enthusiastically supported CBMs in the past, Taipei has also grown increasingly wary of these measures. Although the mainland has frozen political contacts and communications with Taiwan since Tsai's 2016 election, Beijing has permitted continued economic, social and cultural interactions. This includes honouring the 23 cross-strait economic agreements that were signed during Ma's presidency (a CBM of sorts according to the broader understanding of this term).[74] Yet it was precisely these agreements which provoked Taiwanese concerns regarding the island's growing dependence upon the mainland, as evidenced by the Sunflower Movement.

The most significant impediment to new cross-strait CBMs is time. Trust takes years, if not decades, to develop, and the logic of CBMs is thus highly incremental. CBMs are often conceived of as 'building blocks' or 'stepping stones'.[75] Their negotiation and implementation is notoriously slow and often arduous. Yet, as this book has shown, time is of the essence as far as the Taiwan flashpoint is concerned. The risks of a major strategic crisis are growing and will intensify over the next decade. The window for reducing the intense distrust that exists across the Taiwan Strait through incremental CBMs has very likely closed.

This is not to suggest, of course, that there is no basis for agreement between the main parties to this dispute. China, Taiwan and the US each share a common interest in avoiding major conflict at present. Given the risks of inadvertent escalation, they could thus each potentially be convinced to sign onto a set of very specific 'crisis-management' mechanisms designed to pre-empt that possibility. Unlike CBMs, which in their narrowest sense are generally designed to reduce the risk of an accident or miscalculation in the first place, such mechanisms properly seek, in the words of crisis-management scholar David Welch, 'to make it easier for decision makers to contain and resolve confrontations that might occur, unexpectedly or otherwise, between protagonists'.[76]

There is some degree of overlap between CBMs and crisis-management mechanisms. Hotlines, for instance, can both reduce the risk of crises and manage them in the event of escalation. Encouraging Beijing's return to utilising the cross-strait hotline agreed to by Xi and Ma in September 2015 should thus be a priority. But China, Taiwan and the US all need to make efforts to ensure that cross-strait crisis-management mechanisms such as this can survive the early stages of a high-intensity conflict, when their role in managing escalation will arguably be needed most.[77] Beijing and Taipei should also agree upon a set of formal protocols regarding how they would communicate during a major crisis, including back-up procedures should these primary channels fail or get interrupted as the result of a significant military exchange.

Washington's strong encouragement will obviously be critical for the introduction of more robust cross-strait crisis-management mechanisms. But responsibility for this important endeavour should not fall solely to the US. Other countries, such as Japan and Australia, also have much to lose from a cross-strait conflict and should thus lend their support to this effort. Ironically, however, the greatest resistance to going down the path toward more formal and robust crisis-management mechanisms might come from Taiwan. For some time now, Taipei has indicated a preference for a set of largely unspecified 'informal' communication channels which can be utilised during a crisis.[78] As Tsai noted in an interview with the *Washington Post* published in July 2016, her first with a foreign media outlet after becoming president, 'we have always had diverse channels of communications across the strait. These include not just official communications but also people-to-people contacts.'[79]

Such informal channels certainly have their place, as the experience of the October 1962 Cuban Missile Crisis clearly demonstrates. In this classic case of crisis management, informal communications between the Soviet intelligence officer Alexander Fomin and US diplomatic correspondent John Scalie were critical to the final agreement reached by Kennedy and Khrushchev.[80] However, the expansion of the Korean War just over a decade earlier – where Washington failed to pay sufficiently close attention to Chinese anxieties being conveyed through Indian diplomatic intermediaries – highlights how alternatives to more direct forms of diplomatic communication are not without risk.[81]

In the case at hand, these dangers are exacerbated by the fact that there are multiple informal channels for cross-strait communication, including via Taiwan's large business community on the mainland and through KMT–CCP party links. Moreover, in an era where leaders can communicate via text message and where decision-making rarely takes place out of the public eye, the time and relative privacy enjoyed by policy elites during the Cuban Missile Crisis is a luxury unlikely to be afforded today.

Experience also suggests that it might be possible to overcome Chinese reticence towards the establishment of more robust cross-strait crisis-management mechanisms.[82] For almost a decade, Beijing resisted efforts to introduce a Sino-Japanese 'communication mechanism' to reduce the risks of collisions between military ships and aircraft operating in the East China Sea. This initiative included a hotline to connect senior Chinese and Japanese officials in the case of crisis. Beijing was concerned that agreeing to this arrangement would shore up Tokyo's claim to the disputed Senkaku/Diaoyu Islands. However, Beijing's resistance reportedly lessened in 2014 after several 'near misses' involving Chinese and Japanese aircraft operating over the East China Sea.[83] Taiwan would need to be strongly encouraged not to portray the mainland's agreement to more formal crisis mechanisms as reinforcing the island's sovereignty claims. Indeed, given the obvious sensitivities involved, there may even be a case for negotiating the arrangement in secret.

China and the US would also benefit from a set of more clearly defined crisis-management protocols. In the early stages of the EP-3 crisis in April 2001 – which occurred when a US surveillance aircraft collided with a Chinese fighter over the South China Sea – US phone calls to the People's Liberation Army (PLA) headquarters and the Chinese Ministry of Foreign Affairs famously went unanswered. The first diplomatic contact between the two sides did not occur until a full 12 hours following the collision.[84] Some progress has been made towards avoiding a repeat of this episode. At the November 2018 US–China Diplomatic and Security Dialogue, for instance, Washington and Beijing committed to 'developing a military-to-military Crisis Deconfliction and Communication Framework'.[85] This initiative builds upon earlier Sino-American risk-reduction measures, especially two memoranda of understanding that were signed in November 2014: one in which the US and China agreed to notify one another of major military activities; the other a two-part accord regarding rules of behaviour for air and maritime encounters.[86]

The obstacles to developing more robust Sino-American crisis-management mechanisms remain considerable. Beijing's implementation of existing agreements, for instance, has so far been patchy. During the confrontation between the USS *Decatur* and the *Lanzhou* in the South China Sea in September 2018, the Chinese vessel was reportedly not adhering to Code for Unplanned Encounters at Sea (CUES) protocols.[87]

Added to this, the measures agreed to thus far have tended to focus predominantly upon the military-to-military level. While this is obviously an important dimension of crisis management and avoidance, history shows that both civilian and civil–military interactions are equally, if not sometimes more, important. As such, the development and implementation of broader crisis-management mechanisms encompassing both civilian and civil–military interactions will be critical to managing a future Sino-American crisis over Taiwan.[88]

The next stage

Provided the next decade can be navigated successfully, the Taiwan flashpoint could subsequently evolve in a variety of different directions. In 2030, with the spectre of US intervention in a Taiwan contingency substantially diminished, Taipei may opt to sit down with Beijing and to negotiate the best deal it can, albeit with a very weak hand. And even if it does not, Beijing might still be prepared to wait Taipei out, believing that the gravitational pull of the Chinese economy will ultimately draw the island irrevocably into its orbit. Conversely, the mainland might lose patience and initiate military action to resolve the 'Taiwan problem' once and for all.

None of these outcomes, of course, is appealing to Taiwan. Its best hope is that it can augment its military capabilities to the point where Beijing views the costs and risks of military action as outweighing the potential benefits, or that radical political change transpires in China, resulting in the instalment of a more democratic system of government there. While they cannot be written off entirely, neither of these outcomes seems likely based on current trends.

Against this bleak backdrop, the call for crisis-management mechanisms designed essentially to 'muddle through' the coming decade of growing cross-strait instability will appear wholly inadequate to Taiwan's supporters. Yet the alternatives they propose, as well intentioned as these might be, risk a catastrophic conflict that would very likely kill many thousands and drastically change the lives of Taiwan's 23.5 million inhabitants, not to mention undermining broader global economic and strategic stability.

In his magisterial history of strategy, the British scholar Lawrence Freedman concludes that 'strategy is about getting to the next stage rather than some ultimate destination'.[89] Former US secretary of defense Robert McNamara expressed similar sentiment when, in the aftermath of the Cuban Missile Crisis, he observed that 'there is no longer any such thing as strategy, only crisis management'.[90] As they confront this next, potentially dangerous and crisis-riven stage in the enduring Taiwan flashpoint, decision-makers in Beijing, Taipei and Washington must have the prudence and the foresight to recognise this reality.

NOTES

Introduction

1 Robert D. Kaplan, 'A New Cold War Has Begun', *Foreign Policy*, 7 January 2019, https://foreignpolicy.com/2019/01/07/a-new-cold-war-has-begun/amp.

2 Derek Grossman, 'No Smiles Across the Taiwan Strait', *Foreign Policy*, 7 January 2019, https://foreignpolicy.com/2019/01/07/no-smiles-across-the-taiwan-strait.

3 Gerrit van der Wees, 'How President Xi Jinping is Misreading Taiwan', *Diplomat*, 3 January 2019, https://thediplomat.com/2019/01/how-president-xi-jinping-is-misreading-taiwan.

4 Coral Bell, *The Conventions of Crisis: A Study in Diplomatic Management* (Oxford: Oxford University Press for The Royal Institute of International Affairs, 1971), p. 21.

Chapter One

1 June Teufel Dreyer, 'Understanding the Status Quo: Perception and Reality on China-Taiwan Relations', *RUSI Journal*, vol. 152, no. 1, 2007, p. 48.

2 *Ibid.*

3 For a useful overview of Taiwan's early history, see Denny Roy, *Taiwan: A Political History* (Ithaca, NY: Cornell University Press, 2003).

4 Richard C. Bush, *Untying the Knot: Making Peace in the Taiwan Strait* (Washington DC: Brookings Institution Press, 2005), p. 19.

5 *Ibid.*, p. 17.

6 Roy, *Taiwan: A Political History*, pp. 152–79.

7 Bush, *Untying the Knot*, p. 25.

8 Election Study Center, National Chengchi University, 'N.C.C.U., important political attitude trend distribution', 10 July 2019, https://esc.nccu.edu.tw/course/news.php?Sn=166.

9 Stacy Hsu, 'Growing number of Taiwanese willing to go to war against China: poll', Focus Taiwan, 19 July

2019, http://focustaiwan.tw/news/aipl/201907190017.aspx.

10 Marie-Alice McLean-Dreyfus, 'Taiwan: Is there a political generation gap?', *Interpreter*, 9 June 2017, https://www.lowyinstitute.org/the-interpreter/taiwan-there-political-generation-gap.

11 Hsu Szu-chien, 'A Political Profile of Taiwan's Youth: Democratic Support, Natural Independence, and Commitment to Defense', Global Taiwan Institute, 3 April 2018, https://globaltaiwan.org/2018/04/recording-a-political-profile-of-taiwans-youth.

12 'Taiwan's unnerving president does it again', *Economist*, 15 July 1999, https://www.economist.com/asia/1999/07/15/taiwans-unnerving-president-does-it-again.

13 Richard C. Bush, *Uncharted Strait: The Future of China–Taiwan Relations* (Washington DC: Brookings Institution Press, 2012), p. 16.

14 Ko Shu-ling and Charles Snyder, 'Chen says NUC will "cease"', *Taipei Times*, 28 February 2006, http://www.taipeitimes.com/News/front/archives/2006/02/28/2003294988.

15 J. Michael Cole, *Convergence or Conflict in the Taiwan Strait: The Illusion of Peace?* (Abingdon: Routledge, 2017), p. 24.

16 Austin Ramzy, 'When Leaders of Taiwan and China Meet, Even Tiny Gestures Will Be Parsed', *New York Times*, 4 November 2015, https://www.nytimes.com/2015/11/05/world/asia/china-taiwan-xi-jinping-ma-ying-jeou-protocol.html.

17 Cole, *Convergence or Conflict in the Taiwan Strait*, pp. 32–33.

18 See Richard C. Bush, 'Tsai's inauguration in Taiwan: It could have been worse', *Order from Chaos*, Brookings Institution, Washington DC, 23 May 2016, https://www.brookings.edu/blog/order-from-chaos/2016/05/23/tsais-inauguration-in-taiwan-it-could-have-been-worse.

19 Bush, *Uncharted Strait*, p. 12.

20 Bush, 'Tsai's inauguration in Taiwan: It could have been worse'.

21 Charlotte Gao, 'Was it Wise for Tsai Ing-wen to Reject the "1992 Consensus" publicly?', *Diplomat*, 4 January 2019, https://thediplomat.com/2019/01/was-it-wise-for-tsai-ing-wen-to-reject-the-1992-consensus-publicly.

22 Taiwan, Mainland Affairs Council, 'Summarized Results of the Public Opinion Survey on the "Public's View on Current Cross-strait Relations"', August 2018, https://ws.mac.gov.tw/001/Upload/297/relfile/8010/5658/744da024-98b2-443d-82ad-8ba78ba59f9f.pdf.

23 See Fang-Yu Chen, Wei-ting Yen, Austin Horng-en Wang and Brian Hioe, 'The Taiwanese see themselves as Taiwanese, not as Chinese', *Washington Post*, 2 January 2017, https://www.washingtonpost.com/news/monkey-cage/wp/2017/01/02/yes-taiwan-wants-one-china-but-which-china-does-it-want.

24 Richard C. Bush, 'Taiwan's local elections, explained', Brookings Institution, 5 December 2018, https://www.brookings.edu/blog/order-from-chaos/2018/12/05/taiwans-local-elections-explained.

25 Grossman, 'No Smiles Across the Taiwan Strait'.

26 'NSC rolls out "one country, two systems" response measures', *Taiwan Today*, 12 March 2019, https://taiwantoday.tw/news.php?unit=2,6,10,15,18&post=151159.

27 Joseph Yeh, 'China's state-run newspaper "sucks": foreign minister', *Focus Taiwan*, 19 May

2019, http://focustaiwan.tw/news/aipl/201905190007.aspx.

28 'Tsai's moves will only backfire', *China Daily*, 9 August 2018, http://globalchinadaily.com.cn/201808/09/WS5b6b78eaa310add14f384b54.html.

29 Charlie Lyons Jones, 'Taiwan: Tsai Ing-wen's battle to discipline the DPP', *Interpreter*, 8 January 2019, http://www.lowyinterpreter.org/the-interpreter/taiwan-tsai-ing-wen-battle-discipline-dpp.

30 Stacy Hsu, 'Tsai wins DPP primary, beating Lai by 8.2 points', *Focus Taiwan*, 13 June 2019, http://focustaiwan.tw/news/aipl/201906130005.aspx.

31 China, Taiwan Affairs Office and the Information Office of the State Council, 'The One-China Principle and the Taiwan Issue', White Paper, 2000, http://en.people.cn/features/taiwanpaper/Taiwan.html.

32 *Ibid*.

33 For further reading on the first Taiwan Strait crisis of 1954–55, see Robert Accinelli, *Crisis and Commitment: United States Policy Toward Taiwan 1950–1955* (Chapel Hill: University of North Carolina Press, 1996). On the second Taiwan Strait crisis of 1958, see Robert L. Suettinger, 'U.S. "Management" of Three Taiwan Strait "Crises"', in Michael D. Swaine and Zhang Tuosheng, eds, *Managing Sino-American Crises: Case Studies and Analysis* (Washington DC: Carnegie Endowment for International Peace, 2006), pp. 268–76.

34 For an excellent analysis of the evolution of China's Taiwan policy under Mao, see Jing Huang with Xiaoting Li, *Inseparable Separation: The Making of China's Taiwan Policy* (Singapore: World Scientific Publishing Co., 2010), pp. 11–87.

35 *Ibid.*, pp. 106–07.

36 *Ibid.*, p. 41.

37 Susan V. Lawrence and Wayne M. Morrison, 'Taiwan: Issues for Congress', Congressional Research Service Report, 30 October 2017, p. 39.

38 Huang and Li, *Inseparable Separation*, p. 276.

39 'Interview with Wen Jiabao', *Washington Post*, 23 November 2003, https://www.washingtonpost.com/archive/politics/2003/11/23/interview-with-wen-jiabao/1d04cdb0-9b08-4a94-b33a-b978c591525e.

40 Embassy of the People's Republic of China in the United States of America, 'Anti-Secession Law (Full text)', 15 March 2005, http://www.china-embassy.org/eng/zt/999999999/t87406.htm.

41 Denny Roy, *Return of the Dragon: Rising China and Regional Security* (New York: Columbia University Press, 2013), p. 205.

42 Teddy Ng, 'Xi Jinping says efforts must be made to close the China–Taiwan political divide', *South China Morning Post*, 7 October 2013, https://www.scmp.com/news/china/article/1325761/xi-jinping-says-political-solution-taiwan-cant-wait-forever.

43 See Bates Gill and Linda Jakobson, *China Matters: Getting it Right for Australia* (Carlton, Victoria: La Trobe University Press, 2017), p. 17.

44 Cited in Michael Mazza, 'Is a Storm Brewing in the Taiwan Strait?', *Foreign Affairs*, 27 July 2018, https://www.foreignaffairs.com/articles/asia/2018-07-27/storm-brewing-taiwan-strait.

45 Philip Wen and Ben Blanchard, 'Xi warns Taiwan will face "punishment of history" for separatism', Reuters, 20 March 2018, https://www.reuters.

com/article/us-china-parliament-taiwan/xi-warns-taiwan-will-face-punishment-of-history-for-separatism-idUSKBN1GW07X.

46 General Wei Fenghe, State Councilor and Minister of National Defence, China, 'Address to the 18th Asia Security Summit, The IISS Shangri-La Dialogue', 2 June 2019, https://www.iiss.org/events/shangri-la-dialogue/shangri-la-dialogue-2019.

47 China, State Council Information Office, *China's National Defense in the New Era* (Beijing: Foreign Languages Press Co. Ltd, 2019), p. 5.

48 Lawrence Chung, 'Donald Trump's call to Xi Jinping "a relief" for Taiwan', *South China Morning Post*, 11 February 2017, https://www.scmp.com/news/china/diplomacy-defence/article/2069872/taiwan-touch-us-trump-call-xi-jinping.

49 Richard C. Bush, 'A One-China Policy Primer', *East Asia Policy Paper*, no. 10, Center for East Asia Policy Studies at Brookings, March 2017, pp. 6–8, https://www.brookings.edu/wp-content/uploads/2017/03/one-china-policy-primer.pdf.

50 Bush, *Untying the Knot*, p. 17.

51 Man-houng Lin, 'Taiwan's sovereignty status: The neglected Taipei Treaty', in Kimie Hara, ed., *The San Francisco System and Its Legacies* (London: Routledge, 2015), p. 117.

52 Michael J. Green, *By More than Providence: Grand Strategy and American Power in the Asia Pacific since 1783* (New York: Columbia University Press, 2017), p. 274.

53 John Lewis Gaddis, *The Cold War* (London: Allen Lane, 2005), p. 42.

54 Suettinger, 'U.S. "Management" of Three Taiwan Strait "Crises"', p. 257.

55 'Mutual Defence Treaty Between the United States and the Republic of China, 2 December 1954, available at http://avalon.law.yale.edu/20th_century/chin001.asp.

56 Roy, *Taiwan: A Political History*, pp. 150–51.

57 Bush, 'A One-China Policy Primer', p. 10.

58 Reproduced in Alan D. Romberg, *Rein In at the Brink of the Precipice: American Policy Toward Taiwan and U.S.–PRC Relations*, 3rd ed. (Washington DC: The Henry L. Stimson Center, 2003), p. 234.

59 *Ibid.*, p. 238.

60 Steven M. Goldstein and Randall Schriver, 'An Uncertain Relationship: The United States, Taiwan and the Taiwan Relations Act', *China Quarterly*, no. 165, 2001, p. 151.

61 Taiwan Relations Act of 1979, Pub. L. No. 96–98, https://www.congress.gov/bill/96th-congress/house-bill/2479.

62 'Joint Communique of the United States of America and the People's Republic of China (the 1982 Communique)', 17 August 1982, available at https://web-archive-2017.ait.org.tw/en/us-joint-communique-1982.html.

63 For further reading, see Richard Bush, 'The US policy of dual deterrence', in Steve Tsang, ed., *If China Attacks Taiwan: Military Strategy, Politics and Economics* (London: Routledge, 2010), pp. 30–45.

64 Cited in Pan Zhongqi, 'US Taiwan policy of strategic ambiguity: A dilemma of deterrence', *Journal of Contemporary China*, vol. 12, no. 35, 2003, pp. 388–89.

65 For further reading, see Shirley A. Kan, 'Taiwan: Major U.S. Arms Sales Since 1990', Congressional Research Service Report, 29 August 2014, https://fas.org/sgp/crs/weapons/RL30957.pdf.

66 Matt Yu and Evelyn Kao, 'Taiwan welcomes reported shift in U.S. arms sales policy', *Focus Taiwan*, 5 June

2018, http://focustaiwan.tw/news/aipl/201806050026.aspx.

67 Dennis Hickey, 'Taiwan's Security in an Era of Uncertainty', in Shelley Rigger, Dennis V. Hickey and Peter Chow, eds, 'U.S.-Taiwan Relations: Prospects for Security and Economic Ties', Woodrow Wilson International Center for Scholars, April 2017, p. 11, https://www.wilsoncenter.org/sites/default/files/ap_us-taiwan_relations.pdf.

68 Andrew Scobell, 'Show of Force: Chinese Soldiers, Statesmen, and the 1995-1996 Taiwan Strait Crisis', *Political Science Quarterly*, vol. 115, no. 2, Summer 2000, p. 237.

69 J. Michael Cole, 'The Third Taiwan Strait Crisis: The forgotten showdown between China and America', *National Interest*, 10 March 2017, https://nationalinterest.org/feature/the-third-taiwan-strait-crisis-the-forgotten-showdown-19742.

70 For further reading on the 1995–96 crisis, see Nancy Bernkopf Tucker, *United States–Taiwan Relations and the Crisis with China* (Cambridge, MA: Harvard University Press, 2009), pp. 213–50.

71 David E. Sanger, 'U.S. would defend Taiwan, Bush says', *New York Times*, 26 April 2001, https://www.nytimes.com/2001/04/26/world/us-would-defend-taiwan-bush-says.html.

72 Huang and Li, *Inseparable Separation*, p. 276.

73 *Ibid.*, p. 277.

74 *Ibid.*, p. 280.

75 Anna Gearan, Philip Rucker and Simon Denyer, 'Trump's Taiwan phone call was long planned, say people who were involved', *Washington Post*, 4 December 2016, https://www.washingtonpost.com/politics/trumps-taiwan-phone-call-was-weeks-in-the-planning-say-people-who-were-involved/2016/12/04/f8be4b0c-ba4e-11e6-94ac-3d324840106c_story.html.

76 Mark Landler and Michael Forsythe, 'Trump Tells Xi Jinping U.S. Will Honor "One China" Policy', *New York Times*, 9 February 2017, https://www.nytimes.com/2017/02/09/world/asia/donald-trump-china-xi-jinping-letter.html.

77 David Brunnstrom, 'Trump signs U.S.-Taiwan travel bill, angering China', Reuters, 17 March 2018, https://www.reuters.com.article/us-usa-taiwan-china/trump-signs-u-s-taiwan-travel-bill-angering-china-idUSKCN1GS2SN.

78 TS staff, 'The 2019 National Defense Authorization Act: Key Sections on Taiwan and China', 27 July 2018, https://sentinel.tw/the-2019-national-defense-authorization-act-key-sections-on-taiwan-and-china.

79 See, for example, Richard C. Bush, 'The problem with inviting Taiwan's Tsai Ing-wen to speak to a joint meeting of Congress', *Order from Chaos*, Brookings Institution, 8 February 2019, https://www.brookings.edu/blog/order-from-chaos/2019/02/08/the-problem-with-inviting-taiwans-tsai-ing-wen-to-speak-to-a-joint-meeting-of-congress/; and Gerrit van der Wees, 'Why Speaker Pelosi Should Invite President Tsai Ing-wen Before Congress', *Diplomat*, 9 February 2019, https://thediplomat.com/2019/02/why-speaker-pelosi-should-invite-president-tsai-ing-wen-before-congress.

80 Joseph Yeh, 'Tsai, Pelosi phone call no mention of possible US trip: FM', Focus Taiwan, 1 April 2019, http://focustaiwan.tw/aipl/201904010010.aspx.

81 White House, *National Security Strategy of the United States of America*,

Washington DC, December 2017, p. 47, https://www.whitehouse.gov/wp-content/uploads/2017/12/NSS-Final-12-18-2017-0905.pdf.

82 See James Mattis, 'The United States and Asia-Pacific Security', address to the 16th Asia Security Summit', IISS Shangri-La Dialogue, 3 June 2017, from https://www.iiss.org/-/media/images/dialogues/sld/sld-2017/documents/first-plenary-session-as-delivered.ashx; and James Mattis, 'US Leadership and the Challenges of Indo-Pacific security, address to the 17th Asia Security Summit', IISS Shangri-La Dialogue, 2 June 2018, https://www.iiss.org/-/media/images/dialogues/sld/sld-2018/documents/james-mattis-sld18.ashx?la=en&hash=020D1562882D7460CDA17BC67B0037BFE1DDE748.

83 Cited in Chiang Chin-yeh and Joseph Yeh, 'Chinese military provocations won't win Taiwanese hearts: Bolton', Focus Taiwan, 2 April 2019, http://focustaiwan.tw/news/aipl/201904020004.aspx.

84 United States, Department of Defense, Indo-Pacific Strategy Report: Preparedness, Partnerships, and Promoting a Networked Region, 1 June 2019, p. 30.

85 Mike Yeo, 'US State Department OKs license for submarine tech sales to Taiwan', Defense News, 9 April 2018, available from https://www.defensenews.com/naval/2018/04/09/us-state-department-oks-license-for-submarine-tech-sales-to-taiwan.

86 Chris Horton, 'Taiwan Set to Receive $2 Billion in U.S. Arms, Drawing Ire from China', New York Times, 9 July 2019, https://www.nytimes.com/2019/07/09/world/asia/taiwan-arms-sales.html.

87 Edward White and Kathrin Hille, 'US agrees $330m arms sale to bolster Taiwan defences', Financial Times, 25 September 2018, https://www.ft.com/content/43a80396-c05c-11e8-95b1-d36dfe1b89a.

88 Keoni Everington, 'China cries foul at deployment of US soldiers at AIT in Taiwan', Taiwan News, 8 April 2019, https://www.taiwannews.com.tw/en/news/3675448.

89 Teng Pei-ju, 'The new Taiwan-U.S. initiative not an act to provoke Beijing: AIT Director', Taiwan News, 19 March 2019, https://www.taiwannews.com.tw/en/news/3661417.

90 Matthew Strong, 'Taiwan and U.S. National Security chiefs meet for first time since 1979', Taiwan News, 25 May 2019, https://www.taiwannews.com.tw/en/news/3710564.

91 John Power, 'US warships made 92 trips through the Taiwan Strait since 2007', South China Morning Post, 3 May 2019, https://www.scmp.com/week-asia/geopolitics/article/3008621/us-warships-made-92-trips-through-taiwan-strait-2007.

92 'US warship sails through strategic Taiwan Strait amid period of heightened military and economic tension with China', South China Morning Post, 25 July 2019, https://www.scmp.com/news/china/diplomacy/article/3019995/us-warship-sails-through-strategic-taiwan-strait-amid-period.

93 Primrose Riordan, 'Navy frigate tested China's nerve in Taiwan Strait transit', Australian, 18 October 2018, https://www.theaustralian.com.au/national-affairs/defence/navy-frigate-tested-chinas-nerve-in-taiwan-strait-transit/news-story/5c54ce300d6a2c5b5c2b732fbcc20c3c.

94 Ankit Panda, 'Making sense of China's reaction to the French Navy's Taiwan

Strait Transit', *Diplomat*, 27 April 2019, https://thediplomat.com/2019/04/making-sense-of-chinas-reaction-to-the-french-navys-taiwan-strait-transit.

95 Nathan Vanderklippe, 'Canadian warship sails through Taiwan Strait', *Globe and Mail*, 19 June 2019, https://www.theglobeandmail.com/world/article-canadian-warship-sails-through-taiwan-strait.

96 'China changing "status quo", US official warns', *Taipei Times*, 24 March 2019, http://www.taipeitimes.com/News/front/archives/2019/03/24/2003712071.

97 Flor Wang and Wen Kui-hsiang, 'Tsai warns China against altering the status quo', *Focus Taiwan*, 1 April 2019, http://focustaiwan.tw/news/aipl/201904010014.aspx.

Chapter Two

1 International Institute for Strategic Studies, *Military Balance 1979–80* (Oxford: Oxford University Press for the IISS, 1979), pp. 59–61, 64–65.

2 Chong-Pin Lin, 'The Military Balance in the Taiwan Straits', *China Quarterly*, vol. 146, June 1996, p. 579.

3 Ian Easton, *The Chinese Invasion Threat: Taiwan's Defense and American Strategy in Asia* (Arlington, VA: The Project 2049 Institute, 2017), pp. 165–71.

4 See, for example, Stephen W. Bosworth, 'The United States and Asia', *Foreign Affairs*, vol. 71, no. 1, 1991, pp. 113–29.

5 IISS, *The Military Balance 1997* (Oxford: Oxford University Press, 1997/98), p. 167.

6 IISS, *The Military Balance 2019* (Abingdon: Routledge for the IISS, 2019), p. 21.

7 *Ibid.*, p. 307.

8 'Taiwan's Tsai Ing-wen seeks $11 billion defence budget as China threat grows', *Japan Times*, 6 August 2018, https://www.japantimes.co.jp/news/2018/08/06/asia-pacific/taiwans-tsai-ing-wen-seeks-11-billion-defence-budget-china-threat-grows/#.XVaDNOhKiUk.

9 IISS, *The Military Balance 2019*, p. 258.

10 Steven Lee Myers and Chris Horton, 'Once Formidable, Taiwan's Military Now Overshadowed by China's', *New York Times*, 4 November 2017, https://www.nytimes/com/2017/11/04/world/asia/china-taiwan-military.html.

11 Erik Eckholm, 'China Expresses Concern Over Arms Sale to Taiwan', *New York Times*, 25 April 2001, https://www.nytimes.com/2001/04/25/world/china-expresses-concern-over-arms-sale-to-taiwan.html.

12 Questions have been raised over the suitability of Gavron Ltd to oversee the project, including by US officials speaking anonymously and by Taiwanese lawmakers. For further reading, see Teng Pei-ju, 'U.S. official raises doubts about design consultancy firm overseeing new submarine construction', *Taiwan News*, 15 October 2018, https://www.taiwannews.com.tw/en/news/3552735.

13 Lucie Béraud-Sudreau and Joseph Dempsey, 'Indigenous submarines: not quite made in Taiwan?', IISS, 20 August 2018, https://www.iiss.org/blogs/military-balance/2018/08/indigenous-submarines-taiwan; Zachary Keck, 'China's Worst Fear:

Can America Turn Taiwan into a Submarine Power?', *National Interest*, 14 April 2018, https://nationalinterest. org/blog/the-buzz/chinas-worst-fear-can-america-turn-taiwan-submarine-power-25374; and Carl Schuster, 'Here Comes Taiwan's Submarines', *National Interest*, 12 October 2018, https://nationalinterest.org/blog/buzz/here-comes-taiwans-submarines-33391.

14 IISS, *The Military Balance 2019*, pp. 261, 309.

15 David Axe, 'China's J-20 Stealth Fighter Doesn't Need to Be an F-35 to Be Dangerous', *National Interest*, 9 December 2018, https://nationalinterest.org/blog/buzz/chinas-j-20-stealth-fighter-doesn't-need-be-f-35-be-dangerous-38297.

16 Wendell Minnick, 'Taiwan Gives Up on F-35, Turns to F-16V Option', *National Interest*, 28 November 2018, https://nationalinterest.org/blog/buzz/taiwan-gives-f-35-turns-f-16v-option-37332.

17 R.D. Cheng, 'A Median Line in the Taiwan Strait: A Dangerous Loophole', *Taiwan Sentinel*, 3 April 2019, https://sentinel.tw/the-median-line-in-the-taiwan-strait-a-dangerous-loophole.

18 Richard D. Fisher Jr., 'Taiwan reviews its missile programmes', Jane's Intelligence Review, 27 March 2018.

19 For further reading, see Timothy R. Heath, 'China's Untested Military Could Be a Force – or a Flop', *Foreign Policy*, 27 November 2018, https://foreignpolicy.com/2018/11/27/chinas-untested-military-could-be-a-force-or-a-flop.

20 Tim Huxley, 'Why Asia's "arms race" is not quite what it seems', World Economic Forum, 12 September 2018, https://www.weforum.org/agenda/2018/09/asias-arms-race-and-why-it-doesn't-matter.

21 Michael Mazza, 'Taiwan's demographic crunch and its military implications', *Global Taiwan Brief*, vol. 3, no. 2, 24 January 2018, http://globaltaiwan.org/2018/01/24-gtb-3-2/.

22 'For Taiwan youth, military service is a hard sell despite China tension', *Channel NewsAsia*, 29 October 2018, https://www.channelnewsasia.com/news/asia/taiwan-youth-military-service-china-tension-10873554.

23 IISS, *The Military Balance 2019*, p. 256.

24 The application of this term to the Taiwan case is typically attributed to William Murray: see his article 'Revisiting Taiwan's Defense Strategy', *Naval War College Review*, vol. 61, no. 3, Summer 2008, pp. 12–39.

25 Frank Chen, 'Taiwan's small missile boat program hamstrung by budget cuts', *Asia Times*, 13 December 2018, https://cms.ati.ms/2018/12/taiwans-small-missile-boat-program-hamstrung-by-budget-cuts.

26 See, for example, Michael A. Hunzeker and Alexander Lanoszka, *A Question of Time: Enhancing Taiwan's Conventional Deterrence Posture*, Center for Security Policy Studies, Schar School of Policy and Government at George Mason University, November 2018, http://csps.gmu.edu/wp-content/uploads/2018/11/A-Question-of-Time.pdf.

27 J. Michael Cole, 'How Taiwan can defend its coastline against China', *National Interest*, 30 June 2019, https://nationalinterest.org/feature/how-taiwan-can-defend-its-coastline-against-china-64861.

28 Richard Bush, 'The United States Security Partnership with Taiwan', Brookings Order from Chaos series, 13 July 2016, p. 4, https://www.brookings.edu/research/the-united-states-security-partnership-with-taiwan.

29 Eric Heginbotham *et al.*, 'The US-China Military Scorecard: Forces, Geography and the Evolving Balance of Power 1996-2017', RAND Corporation, 2015, p. 333, https://www.rand.org/content/dam/rand/pubs/research_reports/RR300/RR392/RAND_RR392.pdf.

30 For further reading, see Luis Simon, 'Demystifying the A2/AD Buzz', War on the Rocks, 4 January 2017, https://warontherocks.com/2017/01/demystifying-the-a2ad-buzz.

31 See 'Missiles of China', Missile Threat, Center for Strategic and International Studies, https://missilethreat.csis.org/country/china.

32 *Ibid.*

33 Adam Ni and Bates Gill, 'China's New Missile Force: New Ambitions, New Challenges (Part 1)', *Jamestown Foundation China Brief*, vol. 18, no. 14, 10 August 2018, https://jamestown.org/program/chinas-new-missile-force-new-ambitions-new-challenges-part-1.

34 Oriana Skylar Mastro and Ian Easton, 'Risk and Resiliency: China's Emerging Air Base Strike Threat', Project 2049 Institute, 8 November 2017, https://project2049.net/wp-content/uploads/2017/11/P2049_Mastro_Easton_China_Emerging_Airbase_Strike_Threat_110817.pdf.

35 IISS, *The Military Balance 2019*, p. 261.

36 Heginbotham *et al.*, 'US-China Military Scorecard', pp. 82–88.

37 United States, Department of Defense, 'Military and Security Developments Involving the People's Republic of China 2019', May 2019, p. 116, https://media.defense.gov/2018/Aug/16/2001955282/-1/-1/1/2018-CHINA-MILITARY-POWER-REPORT.PDF.

38 Robert Ross, 'The End of U.S. Naval Dominance in Asia', Lawfare, 18 November 2018, https://www.lawfareblog.com/end-us-naval-dominance-asia.

39 US Navy, 'Status of the Navy', 2 August 2019, https://www.navy.mil/navydata/nav_legacy.asp?id=146.

40 See Nick Childs, 'China's naval shipbuilding: delivering on its ambition in a big way', IISS, 1 May 2018, https://www.iiss.org/blogs/military-balance/2018/05/china-naval-shipbuilding.

41 Office of the Secretary of Defense, 'Military and Security Developments Involving the People's Republic of China 2018', p. 30, https://media.defense.gov/2018/Aug/16/2001955282/-1/-1/1/2018-CHINA-MILITARY-POWER-REPORT.PDF.

42 Kyle Mizokami, 'China's Navy: Armed with 4 Aircraft Carriers by 2022?', *National Interest*, 8 November 2018, https://nationalinterest.org/blog/chinas-navy-armed-4-aircraft-carriers-2022-35482.

43 Lyle Goldstein, 'The US-China Naval Balance in the Asia-Pacific: An Overview', *China Quarterly*, vol. 232, December 2017, pp. 904–31, p. 913.

44 *Ibid.*, p. 916.

45 US, Department of Defense, 'China's Military Power 2018', p. 29.

46 Ross, 'The End of U.S. Naval Dominance in Asia'.

47 US, Department of Defense, 'China's Military Power 2018', p. 30.

48 Andrew Erickson, 'Correspondence: How Good Are China's Antiaccess/Area-Denial Capabilities', *International Security*, vol. 41, no. 1, Spring 2017, p. 204.

49 Ross, 'The End of U.S. Naval Dominance in Asia'.

50 Ellen Mitchell, 'Pentagon chief says US looking to put intermediate-range

missiles in Asia', *The Hill*, 3 August 2019, https://thehill.com/policy/defense/456032-pentagon-chief-says-us-looking-to-put-intermediate-range-missiles-in-asia.

51 Heginbotham *et al.*, 'US-China Military Scorecard', p. 327.

52 Cited in Denny Roy, 'Prospects for Taiwan Maintaining Its Autonomy under Chinese Pressure', *Asian Survey*, vol. 57, no. 6, November/December 2017, pp. 1138–39.

53 'China military carries out military exercises in city just opposite Taiwan, days after elections', *Straits Times*, 21 January 2016, https://www.straitstimes.com/east-asia/china-military-carries-out-live-firing-exercises-in-city-just-opposite-taiwan-days.

54 Benjamin Schreer, 'The Double-Edged Sword of Coercion: Cross-Strait Relations After the 2016 Taiwan Elections', *Asian Politics and Policy*, vol. 9, no. 1, 2017, p. 51.

55 Zhang Tao, 'PLA's island encirclement patrols around Taiwan not news anymore', China Military Online, 12 January 2018, http://eng.chinamil.com.cn/view/2018-01/12/content_7907015_2.htm.

56 For further reading, see Derek Grossman *et al.*, 'China's Long-Range Bomber Flights', RAND Corporation, 2018, pp. 20–25.

57 *Ibid.*, p. 23.

58 For further reading, see Murray Scot Tanner, *Chinese Economic Coercion Against Taiwan: A Tricky Weapon to Use*, RAND Corporation, 2007.

59 Kensaku Ihara, 'With economic allure fading, Taiwan keeps its distance from China', *Nikkei Asian Review*, 21 May 2018, https://asia.nikkei.com/Politics/International-Relations/With-economic-allure-fading-Taiwan-keeps-its-distance-from-China.

60 Stratfor, 'Taiwan Confronts the Costs of Economic Integration With Mainland China', Stratfor Worldview, 2 October 2018, https://worldview.stratfor.com/article/taiwan-confronts-costs-economic-integration-mainland-china.

61 Cited in Charlotte Gao, 'Bypassing Tsai Ing-wen, China Offers Perks for Taiwan's People', *Diplomat*, 28 February 2018, https://thediplomat.com/2018/03/bypassing-tsai-ing-wen-china-offers-perks-to-taiwans-people.

62 Simon Denyer, 'Taiwan battles a brain drain as China aims to woo young talent', *Washington Post*, 15 April 2018, https://www.washingtonpost.com/world/asia_pacific/taiwan-battles-a-brain-drain-as-china-aims-to-woo-young-talent-away/2018/04/13/338d096e-3940-11e8-af3c-2123715f78df_story_html.

63 For further reading, see Bonnie S. Glaser, Scott Kennedy and Derek Mitchell, 'The New Southbound Policy: Deepening Taiwan's Regional Integration', Center for Strategic and International Studies, January 2018, https://csis-prod.s3.amazonaws.com/s3fs-public/publication/180113_Glaser_NewSouthboundPolicy_Web.pdf?F5YmxgSJTjWxHCHQr3J88zE.KkzVK5cv.

64 Kelsey Munro, '"Disgusting" and "extraordinary" scenes as Chinese delegation shouts down welcome ceremony', *Sydney Morning Herald*, 2 May 2017, https://www.smh.com.au/politics/federal/disgusting-and-extraordinary-scemes-as-chinese-delegation-shouts-down-welcome-ceremony-20170502-gvxbou.html.

65 'Taiwan accuses World Health Organisation of bowing to Beijing

over invitation to top health meeting', *South China Morning Post*, 8 May 2018, https://sc.mp/2KlaUHr.

66 Goh Sui Noi, 'Taiwan loses third diplomatic ally this year after El Salvador breaks ties', *Straits Times*, 21 August 2018, https://www.straitstimes.com/asia/east-asia/taiwan-set-to-lose-its-third-diplomatic-ally-this-year-source.

67 Gary Sands, 'What the China-Vatican Deal Means for Taiwan', *Diplomat*, 21 September 2018. Available from https://thediplomat.com/2018/09/what-the-china-vatican-deal-means-for-taiwan.

68 Josh Rogin, 'White House calls China's threats to airlines "Orwellian nonsense", *Washington Post*, 5 May 2018, https://www.washingtonpost.com/news/josh-rogin/wp/2018/05/05/white-house-calls-chinas-threats-to-airlines-orwellian-nonsense.

69 Bill Birtles, 'Last remaining US airlines give in to Chinese pressure on Taiwan', ABC News, 25 July 2018, https://www.abc.net.au/news/2018-07-25/us-airlines-give-in-to-chinese-pressure-on-taiwan/10035874.

70 J. Michael Cole, 'China's New Air Routes Near Taiwan: Why Now? To What End?', *Taiwan Sentinel*, 11 January 2018, https://sentinel.yw/analysis-china-new-air-routes-tw.

71 Mark Landler, 'Trump Accuses China of Interfering in Midterm elections', *New York Times*, 26 September 2018, https://www.nytimes.com/2018/09/26/world/asia/trump-china-election.html.

72 For further reading, see Rory Medcalf, 'Australia and China: understanding the reality check', *Australian Journal of International Affairs*, vol. 73, no. 2, 2019, pp. 109–18.

73 Josh Rogin, 'China's interference in the 2018 elections succeeded – in Taiwan', *Washington Post*, 18 December 2018, https://www.washingtonpost.com/opinions/2018/12/18/chinas-interference-elections-succeeded-taiwan.

74 *Ibid.*

75 Hsu, 'Growing number of Taiwanese willing to go to war against China'.

Chapter Three

1 Malcolm Gladwell, *The Tipping Point: How Little Things Can Make a Big Difference* (Boston, MA: Little, Brown, 2000).

2 Josh Rogin, 'China threatens U.S. Congress for crossing its "red line" on Taiwan', *Washington Post*, 12 October 2017, https://www.washingtonpost.com/news/john-rogin/wp/2017/10/12/china-threatens-u-s-congress-for-crossing-its-red-line-on-taiwan.

3 Cited in Kirsty Needham, 'China's live fire drill a "red line" in Taiwan Strait', *Sydney Morning Herald*, 18 April 2018, https://www.smh.com.au/world/asia/china-s-live-fire-drill-a-red-line-in-taiwan-strait-20180418-p4zacf.html.

4 William Kazer, 'China Sets "Red Line" for U.S. Ceremony in Taiwan', *Wall Street Journal*, 10 June 2018, https://www.wsj.com/articles/china-sets-red-line-for-u-s-ceremony-in-taiwan-1528632003?emailToken=6352c475f6dc80ec4edabaf23f142f7bnnVxyO9WcMGn1OcZsNecw4Co23gOID02Ewd6+2kBklPAq5d8lDix0Okx0+kIquq/u007zSFMAy5FN8x0QN3+0/H3k2rMuy86C988hr5L20w%3D&reflink=article_email_share.

5   Scott L. Kastner, 'Is the Taiwan Strait Still a Flash Point? Rethinking the Prospects for Armed Conflict between China and Taiwan', *International Security*, vol. 40, no. 3, Winter 2015/2016, p. 60.

6   Embassy of the People's Republic of China in the United States of America, 'Anti-Secession Law', http://www.chinaembassy.org/eng/zt/999999999/t187406.htm.

7   Cited in Ching-hsin Yu, 'The centrality of maintaining the status quo in Taiwan elections', Brookings, 15 March 2017, https://www.brookings.edu/opinions/the-centrality-of-maintaining-the-status-quo-in-taiwan-elections.

8   *Ibid*.

9   Steve Tsang, 'Drivers Behind the Use of Force', in Steve Tsang, ed., *If China Attacks Taiwan: Military Strategy, Politics and Economics* (London: Routledge, 2006), p. 1.

10 Steven Lee Myers, 'With Xi's Power Grab, China Joins New Era of Strongmen', *New York Times*, 26 February 2018, https://www.nytimes.com/2018/02/26/world/asia/china-xi-jinping-authoritarianism.html.

11 William H. Overholt, 'The West is getting China wrong', *East Asia Forum*, 11 August 2018, http://www.eastasiaforum.org/2018/08/11/the-west-is-getting-china-wrong/

12 For further reading, see Linda Jakobson, 'What does China want?', *Australian Foreign Affairs*, no. 1, October 2017, pp. 50–68.

13 Kastner, 'Is the Taiwan Strait Still a Flash Point?', p. 61.

14 For further reading, see Huang and Li, *Inseparable Separation*.

15 For further reading, see Dennis C. Blair and David V. Bonfili, 'The April 2011 EP-3 Incident: The U.S. Point of View', in Michael D. Swaine and Zhang Tuosheng, eds, *Managing Sino-American Crises* (Washington DC: Carnegie Endowment for International Peace, 2006), pp. 377–90.

16 See Jane Perlez and Steven Lee Myers, 'US and China Are Playing "Game of Chicken" in South China Sea', *New York Times*, 8 November 2018, https://www.nytimes.com/2018/11/08/world/asia/south-china-sea-risks.html. For a more sanguine assessment, see James Goldrick, 'The new normal: a close naval encounter in the South China Sea', *Interpreter*, 9 November 2018, https://www.lowyinstitute.org/the-interpreter/new-normal-close-naval-encounter-south-china-sea.

17 Martin Fackler, 'Japan Says China Aimed Military Radar at Ship', *New York Times*, 5 February 2013, https://www.nytimes.com/2013/02/06/world/asia/japan-china-islnds-dispute.html.

18 Chen Chao-fu and Flor Wang, 'Officer receives reduced sentence in accidental missile launch appeal', *Focus Taiwan*, 7 June 2018, http://focustaiwan.tw/news/asoc/201806070018.aspx.

19 Lawrence Chung and Liu Zhen, 'Taiwan will forcefully expel PLA warplanes next time: Tsai Ing-wen', *South China Morning Post*, 2 April 2019, https://www.scmp.com/news/china/military/article/3004119/chinese-jets-incursion-across-taiwan-strait-beijings-way.

20 See, for example, 'Taiwanese aircraft tail Chinese bombers on flight around island', *South China Morning Post*, 26 May 2018, https://sc.mp/2IJ6wKJ.

21 Kristin Huang, 'Taiwanese pilot "mistakenly fired decoy projectile" in encounter with PLA warplane', *South China Morning Post*, 30 April 2019, https://www.scmp.com/news/china/

military/article/3008320/taiwanese-pilot-mistakenly-fired-decoy-projectile-encouter-pla.

22 Kenneth W. Allen, 'Air Force Deterrence and Escalation Calculations for a Taiwan Strait Conflict: China, Taiwan, and the United States', in Michael D. Swaine, Andrew N.D. Yang and Evan S. Medeiros, eds, *Assessing the Threat: The Chinese Military and Taiwan's Security* (Washington DC: Carnegie Endowment for International Peace, 2007), pp. 169–70.

23 See Cole, 'China's New Air Routes Near Taiwan: Why Now? To What End?'.

24 Allen, 'Air Force Deterrence and Escalation Calculations', p. 170.

25 Liu Chien-pang *et al.*, 'Chinese warship allegedly rams Taiwan cargo vessel off Kinmen', Focus Taiwan, 1 August 2019, http://focustaiwan.tw/news/asoc/201908010013.aspx.

26 Jesse Johnson, 'Taiwan shadows China carrier through narrow strait after warning by Xi: report', *Japan Times*, 21 March 2018, https://www.japantimes.co.jp/news/2018/03/21/asia-pacific/china-dispatches-aircraft-carrier-taiwan-strait-warning-xi-report.

27 Bernard D. Cole, 'The Military Instrument of Statecraft at Sea: Naval Options in an Escalatory Scenario Involving Taiwan: 2007-2016', in Swaine, Yang and Medeiros, *Assessing the Threat*, pp. 185–209.

28 James Holmes, 'Yes, China Could Sink a U.S. Navy Aircraft Carrier. But Don't Bet on It', *National Interest*, 11 January 2019, https://nationalinterest.org/blog/buzz/yes-china-could-sink-us-navy-aircraft-carrier-don't-bet-it-41227.

29 *Ibid.*

30 Barton Gellman, 'U.S. and China nearly came to blows in 96', *Washington Post*, 21 June 1998, https://www.washingtonpost.com/archive/politics/1998/06/21/us-and-china-nearly-came-to-blows-in-96/926d105f-1fd8-404c-9995-90984f86a613.

31 Avery Goldstein, 'First Things First: The Pressing Danger of Crisis Instability in U.S.-China Relations', *International Security*, vol. 37, no. 4, Spring 2013, p. 65.

32 Steven Stashwick, 'South China Sea: Conflict Escalation and "Miscalculation" Myths', *Diplomat*, 25 September 2015, https://thediplomat.com/2015/09/south-china-sea-conflict-escalation-and-miscalculation-myths.

33 Tsang, 'Drivers Behind the Use of Force', p. 3.

34 See Western Pacific Naval Symposium, 'Code for Unplanned Encounters at Sea', 22 April 2014, available at http://www.jag.navy.mil/distrib/instructions/CUES_2014.pdf.

35 Kyodo, 'Japan and China launch defense communication mechanism to prevent air and sea clashes', *Japan Times*, 8 June 2018, https://www.japantimes.co.jp/news/2018/06/08/national/politics-diplomacy/japan-china-launch-defense-communication-mechanism-prevent-air-sea-clashes.

36 Richard Sokolsky, 'North and South Korea Take Important Steps to Demilitarize the Korean Peninsula', 38North, 19 September 2018, https://www.38north.org/2018/09/rsokolsky091918.

37 Song Jung-a, 'Korean leaders establish phone hotline ahead of summit', *Financial Times*, 20 April 2018, https://www.ft.com/content/df5204a0-4482-11e8-803a-295c97e6fd0b.

38 'Taiwan, China launch hotline after historic summit', *Straits Times*, 30 December 2015, https://www.

straitstimes.com/asia/east-asia/taiwan-china-launch-hotline-after-historic-summit.

[39] IISS, 'Turbulence in the Taiwan Strait', *Strategic Comments*, August 2016, https://www.iiss.org/publications/strategic-comments/2019/tensions-in-the-taiwan-strait.

[40] Allen, 'Air Force Deterrence and Escalation Calculations for a Taiwan Strait Conflict', pp. 170–71.

[41] See, for example, Aaron L. Friedberg, 'Competing with China', *Survival: Global Politics and Strategy*, vol. 60, no. 3, June–July 2018, pp. 7–64; and Robert D. Kaplan, 'A New Cold War Has Begun', *Foreign Policy*, 7 January 2019, https://foreignpolicy.com/2019/01/07/a-new-cold-war-has-begun/amp.

[42] Jane Perlez, 'Pence's China Speech Seen as Portent of "New Cold War"', *New York Times*, 5 October 2018, https://www.nytimes.com/2018/10/05/world/asia/pence-china-speech-cold-war.html.

[43] 'Vice President Mike Pence's Remarks on the Administration's Policy Towards China', Hudson Institute, 4 October 2018, https://www.hudson.org/events/1610-vice-president-mike-pence-s-remarks-on-the-administration-s-policy-towards-china102018.

[44] Chris Horton, Lauly Li and Cheng Ting-fang, 'Trade war traps Taiwan between two superpowers', *Nikkei Asian Review*, 5 December 2018, https://asia.nikkei.com/Spotlight/Cover-Story/Trade-war-traps-Taiwan-between-two-superpowers.

[45] Richard C. Bush, 'What Taiwan can take from Mike Pence's speech on China', Brookings Institution, 12 October 2018, http://www.brookings.edu/blog/order-from-chaos/2018/10/12/what-taiwan-can-take-from-mike-pences-speech-on-china.

[46] For further reading, see Suettinger, 'U.S. "Management" of Three Taiwan Strait "Crises"', pp. 251–76.

[47] For further reading, see Iain Donald Henry, *Reliability and Alliance Politics: Interdependence and America's Asian Alliance System*, PhD Dissertation, Australian National University, Canberra, 2017.

[48] Ankit Panda, 'Obama: Senkakus Covered Under US-Japan Security Treaty', *Diplomat*, 24 April 2014, https://thediplomat.com/2014/04/obama-senkakus-covered-under-us-japan-security-treaty.

[49] Ayako Mie, 'Mattis clarifies U.S. defense pledge, stays mum on host-nation support', *Japan Times*, 4 February 2017, https://www.japantimes.co.jp/news/2017/02/04/national/politics-diplomacy/mattis-clarifies-u-s-defense-pledge-stays-mum-host-nation-support.

[50] See, for example, Nancy Bernkopf Tucker and Bonnie Glaser, 'Should the United States Abandon Taiwan?', *Washington Quarterly*, vol. 34, no. 4, Fall 2011, pp. 32–33.

[51] For further reading, see Suettinger, 'U.S. "Management" of Three Taiwan Strait "Crises"', pp. 276–86.

[52] Cited in James R. Holmes and Toshi Yoshihara, *Chinese Naval Strategy in the 21st Century: The Turn to Mahan* (Abingdon: Routledge, 2008), p. 94.

[53] Roy, *Taiwan*, p. 108.

[54] See, for instance, Seth Cropsey, 'Taiwan is key to US power in Pacific', *The Hill*, 17 August 2018, https://thehill.com/opinion/national-security/402286-Taiwan-is-key-to-US-power-in-Pacific.

[55] Roy, *Return of the Dragon*, p. 209.

56 Thomas G. Mahnken, 'Cost-Imposing Strategies: A Brief Primer', Center for a New American Security, Washington DC, November 2014, p. 6, https://s3.amazonaws.com/files.cnas.org/documents/CNAS_Maritime4_Mahnken.pdf?mtime=20160906081628.

57 Henry Kissinger, *On China* (London: Allen Lane, 2011), p. 153.

58 David Spencer, 'Taiwan has other deterrence options besides costly and controversial nuclear weapons', *Taiwan News*, April 2019, https://www.taiwannews.com.tw/en/news/3673904.

59 David C. Kang, 'Getting Asia Wrong: The Need for New Analytical Frameworks', *International Security*, vol. 27, no. 4, Spring 2003, pp. 57–85.

60 James Curran, 'Australia cannot afford to be distracted by the cold war talk', *Australian*, 24 November 2018, https://www.theaustralian.com.au/news/inquirer/australia-cannot-afford-to-be-distracted-by-the-cold-war-talk/news-story/2421bbdd112d0db7629514c46d23cd90.

61 Caitlin Talmadge, 'Would China Go Nuclear? Assessing the Risk of Chinese Nuclear Escalation in a Conventional War with the United States', *International Security*, vol. 41, no. 4, Spring 2017, p. 76.

62 Goldstein, 'First Things First', pp. 69–70.

63 Talmadge, 'Would China Go Nuclear?', p. 75.

64 Caitlin Talmadge, 'Beijing's Nuclear Option', *Foreign Affairs*, 15 October 2018, https://www.foreignaffairs.com/articles/china/2018-10-15/beijings-nuclear-option.

65 Dennis C. Blair, 'Would China Go Nuclear?', *Foreign Affairs*, 11 December 2018, https://www.foreignaffairs.com/articles/2018-12-11/would-china-go-nuclear.

66 *Ibid.*

67 United States, Defense Intelligence Agency, 'China Military Power: Modernizing a Force to Fight and Win', 2019, p. 40, https://www.dia.mil/Portals/27/Documents/News/Military%20Power%20Publications/China_Military_Power_FINAL_5MB_20190103.pdf.

68 Goldstein, 'First Things First', p. 67.

69 For further reading, see David C. Gompert and Martin Libicki, 'Cyber Warfare and Sino-American Crisis Instability', *Survival: Global Politics and Strategy*, vol. 56, no. 4, August–September 2014, pp. 7–22.

70 Robert Ayson and Desmond Ball, 'Can a Sino-Japanese War Be Controlled?', *Survival: Global Politics and Strategy*, vol. 56, no. 6, December 2014–January 2015, p. 153.

71 For further reading, see James R. Holmes, 'The Sino-Japanese Naval War of 2012', *Foreign Policy*, 20 August 2012, https://foreignpolicy.com/2012/08/20/the-sino-japanese-naval-war-of-2012.

72 See, for example, 'Military tensions on the rise in the Taiwan Strait', *Japan Times*, 7 April 2019, https://www.japantimes.co.jp/opinion/2019/04/07/editorials/military-tensions-rise-taiwan-strait.

73 For further reading, see Jeffrey W. Hornung, 'Strong but constrained Japan-Taiwan ties', Brookings Institution, 13 March 2018, https://www.brookings.edu/opinions/strong-but-constrained-japan-taiwan-ties.

Chapter Four

1   Victor Cha, *The Impossible State: North Korea, Past and Future* (New York: HarperCollins, 2012), p. 246.

2   Noah Bierman, 'Trump warns North Korea of "fire and fury"', *Los Angeles Times*, 8 August 2017, https://www.latimes.com/politics/washington/la-na-essential-washington-updates-trump-warns-north-korea-of-fire-and-1502220642-htmlstory.html.

3   Kent Wang, 'A Peace Agreement Between China and Taiwan?', *Diplomat*, 5 September 2013, https://thediplomat.com/2013/09/a-peace-agreement-between-china-and-taiwan.

4   David G. Brown and Kevin Scott, 'China Increases Pressure, Tsai Holds the Line', *Comparative Connections*, vol. 19, no. 2, September 2017, p. 68.

5   'Taiwan's KMT signals peace treaty with Beijing', *Asia Times*, 15 February 2019, https://www.asiatimes.com/2019/02/article/taiwans-kmt-signals-peace-treaty-with-beijing.

6   For an excellent discussion envisioning the different forms a China–Taiwan peace agreement might take, see Phillip C. Saunders and Scott L. Kastner, 'Bridge over Troubled Water? Envisioning a China-Taiwan Peace Agreement', *International Security*, vol. 33, no. 4, Spring 2009, pp. 91–98.

7   *Ibid.*, pp. 103–07.

8   'Taiwan's pro-independence government seeks peace accord with China', *Kyodo News*, 3 November 2016.

9   See 'DPP Resolution on Taiwan's Future', Kaohsiung, 8 May 1999, http://www.taiwandc.org/nws-9920.htm.

10 'Taiwan warns opposition against signing agreements with China', EFE News Service, 27 October 2016.

11 Yu Hsiang and Evelyn Kao, 'Cross-strait peace pact bill not targeted at any person: Premier', *Focus Taiwan*, 19 February 2019, http://focustaiwan.tw/news/aipl/201902190015.aspx.

12 Saunders and Kastner, 'Bridge over Troubled Water?', p. 107.

13 Gerard Gayou, 'Xi's Promise to Taiwan Sounds Like a Threat', *Wall Street Journal*, 4 January 2019, https://www.wsj.com/articles/xis-promise-to-taiwan-sounds-like-a-threat-11546559725.

14 Richard C. Bush, *Hong Kong in the Shadow of China: Living with the Leviathan* (Washington DC: Brookings Institution Press, 2016), p. 226.

15 *Ibid.*, pp. 223–27.

16 *Ibid.*, p. 232.

17 Ben Bland, 'Hong Kong: is "one country, two systems" under threat?', *Financial Times*, 3 December 2018, https://www.ft.com/content/43a34a48-f16e8-9623-d7f9881e729f.

18 Chris Horton, 'Hong Kong and Taiwan are bonding over China', *Atlantic*, 5 July 2019, https://www.theatlantic.com/international/archive/2019/07/china-bonds-between-hong-kong-and-taiwan-are-growing/593347.

19 Stacy Hsu, 'Over 80% reject "two systems", poll finds', *Taipei Times*, 10 January 2019, http://www.taipeitimes.com/News/front/archives/2019/01/10/2003707656.

20 Kris Cheng, 'Fewer Hongkongers see "One Country, Two Systems" as applicable to Taiwan – survey', *Hong Kong Free Press*, 24 January 2019, https://www.hongkongfp.com/2019/01/24/fewer-hongkongers-see-one-country-two-systems-applicable-taiwan-survey/.

21 Cited in Chris Horton, 'Taiwan's President, Defying Xi Jinping, Calls Unification Offer "Impossible"', *New York Times*, 5 January 2019, https://nytimes.com/2019/01/05/world/asia/taiwan-xi-jinping-tsai-ing-wen.html.

22 'Tsai Ing-wen's prospects for re-election have improved', *Economist*, 27 July 2019, https://www.economist.com/asia/2019/07/27/tsai-ing-wens-prospects-for-re-election-have-improved.

23 Peter Nicholas, Paul Beckett and Gerald F. Seib, 'Trump Open to Shift on Russia Sanctions, "One China" Policy', *Wall Street Journal*, 13 January 2017, https://www.wsj.com/articles/donald-trump-sets-a-bar-for-russia-and-china-1484360380.

24 See, for example, Adam Taylor, 'With Trump in China, Taiwan worries about becoming a "bargaining chip"', *Washington Post*, 9 November 2017, https://www.washingtonpost.com/world/with-trump-in-china-taiwan-worries-about-becoming-abargaining-chip/2017/11/09/ee3c0126-c4af-11e7-9922-4151f5ca6168_story.html.

25 Bob Woodward, *Fear: Trump in the White House* (New York: Simon & Schuster, 2018), p. 305.

26 For further reading, see Nancy Bernkopf Tucker, 'Taiwan Expendable? Nixon and Kissinger Go to China', *Journal of American History*, vol. 92, no. 1, June 2005, pp. 109–35.

27 Charles L. Glaser, 'A US-China Grand Bargain? The Hard Choice between Military Competition and Accommodation', *International Security*, vol. 39, no. 4, Spring 2015, pp. 49–90.

28 Lyle J. Goldstein, *Meeting China Halfway: How to Defuse the Emerging US–China Rivalry* (Washington DC:

Georgetown University Press, 2015), pp. 46–78.

29 Sherry Hsiao, 'US House passes Taiwan Assurance Act', *Taipei Times*, 9 May 2019, http://www.taipeitimes.com/News/front/archives/2019/05/09/2003714812.

30 Aaron L. Friedberg, 'Will We Abandon Taiwan?', *Commentary*, May 2000, https://www.commentarymagazine.com/articles/will-we-abandon-taiwan.

31 For a useful summary of the arguments against lessening the US security commitment to Taiwan, see Bernkopf, Tucker and Glaser, 'Should the United States Abandon Taiwan?', pp. 23–37.

32 For further reading on the history of Taiwan's nuclear programme, see Mark Fitzpatrick, *Asia's Latent Nuclear Powers: Japan, South Korea and Taiwan* (London: Routledge for the IISS, 2015), pp. 127–34; and Kyle Mizokami, 'China's Worst Nightmare: Imagine If Taiwan Had Nuclear Weapons', *National Interest*, 19 April 2018, https://nationalinterest.org/blog/the-buzz/chinas-worst-nightmare-imagine-if-taiwan-had-nuclear-weapons-25463.

33 Eric Gomez, 'A Costly Commitment: Options for the Future of the U.S.-Taiwan Defense Relationship', Cato Institute, 28 September 2016, p. 5, https://www.cato.org/publications/policy-analysis/costly-commitment-options-future-us-taiwan-defense-relationship.

34 Cited in Julian G. Ku, 'America Just Quietly Backed Down Against China Again', *Foreign Policy*, 29 November 2017, https://foreignpolicy.com/2017/11/29/america-just-quietly-backed-down-against-china-again.

35 Cited in John Pomfret, 'Can China really take over Taiwan?', *Washington Post*, 5 January 2018, https://

www.washingtonpost.com/news/global-opinions/wp/2018/01/05/can-china-really-take-over-taiwan.

36 See, for example, Michael S. Chase, 'Averting a Cross-Strait Crisis', Council on Foreign Relations, 26 February 2019, https://www.cfr.org/report/averting-cross-strait-crisis.

37 Richard L. Armitage, Ian Easton and Mark Stokes, 'U.S.-Taiwan Relations in a Sea of Change: Navigating Toward a Brighter Future', Project 2049 Institute, March 2018, p. 26.

38 See, for example, Michael Mazza and Gary Schmitt, 'The F-35: How Taiwan Could Really Push Back Against China', National Interest, 18 January 2018, https://nationalinterest.org/blog/the-buzz/the-f-35-how-taiwan-could-really-push-back-against-china-24127.

39 Joseph Bosco, 'Time to Let Taiwan Join the Pacific Partnership', Diplomat, 27 February 2018, https://thediplomat.com/2018/02/time-to-let-taiwan-join-the-pacific-partnership.

40 'The 2019 National Defense Authorization Act: Key Sections on Taiwan and China', Taiwan Sentinel, 27 July 2018, https://sentinel.tw/the-2019-national-defense-authorization-act-key-sections-on-taiwan-and-china.

41 See Chase, 'Averting a Cross-Strait Crisis'.

42 Daniel Blumenthal and Michael Mazza, 'A Golden Opportunity for a U.S.-Taiwan Free Trade Agreement', Project 2049 Institute, 14 February 2019, pp. 4–5.

43 See Chase, 'Averting a Cross-Strait Crisis'.

44 Hugh White, 'Taiwan: US deterrence is failing', Interpreter, 22 May 2015, https://www.lowyinstitute.org/the-interpreter/taiwan-us-detrerrence-failing.

45 See Anna Gearan and Karoun Demirjian, 'Trump vowed to leave Syria in a tweet. Now, with a Sharpie, he agreed to stay', Washington Post, 5 March 2019, https://www.washingtonpost.com/politics/in-reversal-on-syria-trump-tells-lawmakers-he-agrees-100-percent-that-some-us-forces-should-stay/2019/03/05/c8fcfe9e-3f7c-11e9-a0d3-1210e58a94cf_story.html; and Henry Olsen, 'Trump has given North Korea a valuable bargaining chip for free', Washington Post, 5 March 2019, https://www.washingtonpost.com/opinions/2019/03/05/trump-has-given-north-korea-valuable-bargaining-chip-free.

46 Ross, 'The End of U.S. Naval Dominance in Asia'.

47 Gomez, 'A Costly Commitment', p. 10.

48 Robert S. Ross, 'Navigating the Taiwan Strait: Deterrence, Escalation Dominance, and U.S.-China Relations', International Security, vol. 27, no. 2, Fall 2002, p. 53.

49 Stephan Fruhling, 'US strategy: between the "pivot" and "Air-Sea Battle"', East Asia Forum, 26 August 2012, https://www.eastasiaforum.org/2012/08/26/us-strategy-between-the-pivot-and-air-sea-battle.

50 Benjamin Katzeff Silberstein, 'China Sanctions Enforcement and Fuel Prices in North Korea: What the Data Tells Us', 38 North, 1 February 2019, https://www.38north.org/2019/02/bkatzeffsilberstein020119.

51 Richard D. Fisher, Jr., 'Taiwan reviews its missile programmes', Jane's Intelligence Review, 27 March 2018.

52 Ian Easton, 'China's Top Five War Plans', Project 2049 Institute, 6 January 2019, https://project2049.net/2019/01/06/chinas-top-five-war-plans.

53 Ian Easton, *The Chinese Invasion Threat: Taiwan's Defense and American Strategy in Asia* (Arlington, VA: The Project 2049 Institute, 2017), pp. 99–100.

54 Michael Beckley, 'The Emerging Military Balance in East Asia: How China's Neighbors Can Check Chinese Naval Expansion', *International Security*, vol. 42, no. 2, Fall 2017, p. 91.

55 *Ibid.*

56 Easton, *The Chinese Invasion Threat*, p. 102.

57 For further reading, see *Ibid.*, pp. 114–21.

58 Tanner Greer, 'Taiwan Can Win a War With China', *Foreign Policy*, 25 September 2018, https://foreignpolicy.com/2018/09/25/taiwan-can-win-a-war-with-china.

59 Easton, *The Chinese Invasion Threat*, p. 206.

60 *Ibid.*, p. 207.

61 *Ibid.*, pp.135–36.

62 Denny Roy, "Prospects for Taiwan Maintaining Its Autonomy under Chinese Pressure', *Asian Survey*, vol. 57, no. 6, 2017, pp. 1135–58, p. 1141.

63 Beckley, 'The Emerging Military Balance in East Asia', p. 92.

64 *Ibid.*, p. 94.

65 David C. Gompert, Astrid Smith Cevallos and Christina L. Garafold, *War with China: Thinking Through the Unthinkable* (Santa Monica, CA: RAND Corporation, 2016).

66 *Ibid.*, pp. 41–50.

67 *Ibid.*

68 For further reading, see Bonnie S. Glaser, 'Cross-Strait Confidence Building: The Case for Military Confidence-Building Measures', in Donald S. Zagoria, ed., *Breaking the China-Taiwan Impasse* (Westport, CT: Praeger, 2003), pp. 157–63.

69 *Ibid.*, p. 177.

70 For a useful summary of previous cross-strait CBMs, see Brad Glosserman, 'Cross-Strait Confidence Building Measures', *Issues & Insights*, vol. 5, no. 2, February 2005, pp. 7–16.

71 *Ibid.*, pp. 11–13.

72 Bonnie Glaser and Brad Glosserman, 'Promoting Confidence Building across the Taiwan Strait', A Report of the CSIS International Security Program and Pacific Forum CSIS, September 2008, p. 13.

73 See Glaser, 'Cross-Strait Confidence Building', p. 177; and Glaser and Glosserman, 'Promoting Confidence Building across the Taiwan Strait', pp. 14–19.

74 Bonnie Glaser, 'Managing Cross-Strait Ties in 2017', Center for Strategic and International Studies, January 2017, p. 6, https://www.csis.org/analysis/managing-cross-strait-ties-2017.

75 Glosserman, 'Cross-Strait Confidence Building Measures', p. 7.

76 David A. Welch, 'Crisis Management Mechanisms: Pathologies and Pitfalls', *CIGI Papers*, no. 40, September 2014, p. 5.

77 For further reading, see Desmond Ball, 'Improving Communications Links between Moscow and Washington', *Journal of Peace Research*, vol. 28, no. 2, May 1991, pp. 135–59.

78 See Glaser and Glosserman, 'Promoting Confidence Building across the Taiwan Strait', p. 12. This same logic was reiterated during more recent discussions with senior Taiwanese officials in Taipei conducted as part of this project.

79 Lally Weymouth, 'Taiwanese President Tsai Ing-wen: Beijing must respect our democratic will', *Washington Post*, 21 July 2016, https://www.washingtonpost.com/

opinions/2016/07/21/44b0a1a4-4e25-11e6-a422-83ab49ed5e6a_story.html.

80 Phil Williams, *Crisis Management: Confrontation and Diplomacy in the Nuclear Age* (New York: John Wiley & Sons, 1976), p. 190.

81 *Ibid.*, p. 185.

82 For an excellent discussion of the evolution of Chinese approaches to crisis management, see Alastair Iain Johnston, 'The Evolution of Interstate Security Crisis-Management Theory and Practice in China', *Naval War College Review*, vol. 69, no. 1, Winter 2016, pp. 29–71.

83 International Crisis Group, 'East China Sea: Preventing Clashes from Becoming Crises', *Asia Report*, no. 280, 30 June 2016, p. 8.

84 Blair and Bonfili, 'The April 2001 EP-3 Incident', p. 380.

85 US, Department of State, 'U.S.-China Diplomatic and Security Dialogue', 9 November 2018, https://www.state.gov/r/pa/prs/ps/2018/11/287282.htm.

86 For further reading, see Ashley Townsend and Rory Medcalf, 'Shifting waters: China's new passive assertiveness in Asian maritime security', Lowy Institute for International Policy, April 2016, pp. 30–31.

87 Michael Fabey, 'Confrontation between Chinese and US destroyers suggests policy shift', Jane's Navy International, 4 October 2018, https://www.janes.com/article/83571/confrontation-between-chinese-and-us-destroyers-suggests-policy-shift.

88 Michael D. Swaine, 'A Relationship Under Extreme Duress: U.S.-China Relations at a Crossroads', Carnegie Endowment for International Peace, Washington DC, 16 January 2019, https://carnegieendowment.org/2019/01/16/relationship-under-extreme-duress-u.s.-china-relations-at-crossroads-pub-78159.

89 Lawrence Freedman, *Strategy: A History* (Oxford and New York: Oxford University Press, 2013), p. 628.

90 Cited in Coral Bell, *The Conventions of Crisis* (London, Oxford and New York: Oxford University Press for the Royal Institute of International Affairs, 1971), p. 2.

INDEX

Adelphi books are published six times a year by Routledge Journals, an imprint of Taylor & Francis, 4 Park Square, Milton Park, Abingdon, Oxfordshire OX14 4RN, UK.

A subscription to the institution print edition, ISSN 1944-5571, includes free access for any number of concurrent users across a local area network to the online edition, ISSN 1944-558X. Taylor & Francis has a flexible approach to subscriptions enabling us to match individual libraries' requirements. This journal is available via a traditional institutional subscription (either print with free online access, or online-only at a discount) or as part of our libraries, subject collections or archives. For more information on our sales packages please visit www.tandfonline.com/page/librarians.

2019 Annual Adelphi Subscription Rates			
Institution	£785	US$1,376	€1,451
Individual	£269	US$460	€368
Online only	£667	US$1,170	€986

Dollar rates apply to subscribers outside Europe. Euro rates apply to all subscribers in Europe except the UK and the Republic of Ireland where the pound sterling price applies. All subscriptions are payable in advance and all rates include postage. Journals are sent by air to the USA, Canada, Mexico, India, Japan and Australasia. Subscriptions are entered on an annual basis, i.e. January to December. Payment may be made by sterling cheque, dollar cheque, international money order, National Giro, or credit card (Amex, Visa, Mastercard).

For a complete and up-to-date guide to Taylor & Francis journals and books publishing programmes, and details of advertising in our journals, visit our website: **http://www.tandfonline.com**.

Ordering information:
USA/Canada: Taylor & Francis Inc., Journals Department, 530 Walnut Street, Suite 850, Philadelphia, PA 19106, USA. **UK/Europe/Rest of World:** Routledge Journals, T&F Customer Services, T&F Informa UK Ltd., Sheepen Place, Colchester, Essex, CO3 3LP, UK.

Advertising enquiries to:
USA/Canada: The Advertising Manager, Taylor & Francis Inc., 530 Walnut Street, Suite 850, Philadelphia, PA 19106, USA. Tel: +1 (800) 354 1420. Fax: +1 (215) 207 0050. **UK/Europe/Rest of World**: The Advertising Manager, Routledge Journals, Taylor & Francis, 4 Park Square, Milton Park, Abingdon, Oxfordshire OX14 4RN, UK. Tel: +44 (0) 20 7017 6000. Fax: +44 (0) 20 7017 6336.